Reaching Rahab

Reaching Rahab

JOINING GOD IN HIS QUEST FOR FRIENDS

Barney Wiget

© 2018 Barney Wiget
All rights reserved.

ISBN: 1981704698
ISBN 13: 9781981704699
Library of Congress Control Number: 2018900362
CreateSpace Independent Publishing Platform
North Charleston, South Carolina

"'Love God, love people, and make disciples. Lovers of God love people toward becoming God lovers themselves.' This is what this book is all about. It takes us beyond the technique of 'friendship evangelism' into 'making friends with God.' Barney often street preaches outside our YWAM building in the tough streets of the Tenderloin. But more than preach, I always see him before and after he preaches engaging, dialoging and making friends with the people on the street.

"Barney's evangelism flows out of a brokenness that helps him to relate to people as a friend, a fellow learner and one who can relate with empathy in people's personal journey. He shares many practical stories, lessons and insights in this book to help us on the road to be better friends and coaches with those who are on the road to an encounter with Jesus. All the chapters in this book are practical and down to earth on how we as God's people can be lovers of people leading them to love God with us."
—**Tim Svoboda,** YWAM San Francisco Bay Area Coordinator

"This book is a keeper! It should be placed in the hands of every believer and taught as a course in every local church, because it has the power to not only deeply inform new believers about the simplicity of sharing their faith but to ignite the hearts of "older brothers and sisters" who have lost the spark of their early days of re-birth. The world is full of "Rahabs" waiting for God's spies to do their part. Barney's book will help them get there without all the gobbledegook of religious methodologies. Go spies!"
—**Ron Pinkston,** longtime Pastor and Supervisor of Central Pacific District of Foursquare Churches

"For those of us who are reluctant evangelists, Barney Wiget has offered a great gift in his book, 'Reaching Rahab.' With his characteristically accessible style, solid scholarship, and deeply spiritual insights, he welcomes us to trade our heavy-handed, guilt-polluted approaches for the adventure of 'Joining God in His Quest for Friends.' And then, using the very familiar but under-explored example of the rescue of a Jericho prostitute, he shows us how. Wiget uses a highly-practical, step-by-step approach as he guides us along a biblical template for sharing our faith without making it formulaic. Instead, we find ourselves discovering a much more natural and powerful way of living in this world as bearers of the Good News."

—**Randy Boldt,** veteran Church Planter and Pastor

"Guilt–free, refreshing, captivating, and real! The introduction alone is a good practical theology text on evangelism. It will help to bring the Body of Christ back to what is important: know the friendship of Jesus and bring our friend Jesus to the world. Barney lovingly and insightfully provides a pathway of a Jesus style and substantive evangelism."

—**Rick Wulfestieg,** founding Executive Director of Foursquare Media

"I've known Barney Wiget for more than thirty years. His passion for Jesus is honest and his love for introducing him to others is contagious. In his second book, Reaching Rahab, we get to see the story of God's redemption played out through a variety of processes that Barney highlights. He draws on his own prolific personal experiences of befriending people and introducing them to the person of Jesus. He uses the story of Rahab as a diamond in the light, turning the story to reveal the many ways God draws people to him through our daily encounters that can turn into honest friendships. This is not a book about methodology, nor is it evangelism 101. This is inspiration to find freedom in expressing your own love for Jesus with others in a way that is uniquely you. Rahab is the story, Barney the interpreter, and a lifetime of

personal experiences are the inspiration to find freedom in life's journey to find your own unique path in fulfilling our one great purpose: to love God and to love people toward him."
—**Randy Finkbeiner,** Missionary to KwaMhlanga, South Africa

Is there a way for us to help our friends understand the good news in a fresh and inspiring way? The answer is "yes" and Barney does just that in this book. He provides a new way of seeing how God is already at work and how we can participate with Him as they come into a fuller relationship with Him. Reading this book, you will be inspired again to stir up the good-news gift in your own heart. Get ready to start sharing again!
—**Stuart Nice,** Pastor and Private School Principal

To my granddaughters, Aria Joy Davis and Esmé Davi Wiget, whose generation, I predict, will need Jesus even more than my own.

Table of Contents

Introduction ·· xv

    Don't Fight the Force ································ xv

    The Friendship Quest ································ xviii

    Expertise Not Required ······························ xxii

    Reaching Rahab ······································ xxiv

PART ONE **A Supernaturally Installed Wonder** ·················· 1

    God's Passionate Pursuit of People ···················· 7

    She Sees God in Creation ····························· 12

    She Sees God in Her Conscience ······················ 15

    She Sees God in Her Culture ·························· 18

    She Sees God in Her Crises ··························· 21

        She Sees God in Her Creed ··························· 25

        Enter – A Pair of "Witnesses" ························ 29

        We'll Take That "To Go" ······························ 33

PART TWO Accidental Evangelism ···················· 41

        The Wordless Witness ································ 47

        The Disarming Power of Reluctant Humility ··········· 56

        Sometimes Less is More ······························ 60

PART THREE It Takes a Savior To Save ················ 65

        Savior Sellers? ······································· 71

        Winning, Not Wounding ······························· 75

        Sometimes Do and Sometimes Don't ·················· 85

        The "Jesus Bus" ······································ 91

        Rahab's Redemptive Red Rope ······················· 97

PART FOUR Befriending the Prostituted ·············· 103

        Humanizing the Dehumanized ······················· 109

        Re-earning Trust ···································· 115

        Mutualizing the Marginalized ······················· 121

Outer Circle Christians · 125

Squeezing Camels · 132

Rethinking Our Testimony · 139

CONCLUSION **One Thing Leads To Another** · 145

Recommended Reading · 151

For Personal Reflection, Group Discussion, and Taking Action · 155

Acknowledgements · 173

About the Author · 175

Notes · 177

Introduction

Don't Fight the Force

As a child I had a semi-harmless addiction to merry-go-rounds. It was always the first thing I ran to when unleashed on a playground. "Faster!" I shouted to whoever was willing to push as my face turned blue and my stomach queased. For me the game was resisting the increasing centrifugal force pushing outward by fighting my way to the center. I found it surreal that in the middle I could no longer feel the force pushing me outward. I'm sure there's some science to it – something about Newton and a law he made up – but all I knew at the time was I had won the battle against the merry-go-round, usually at the price of near vomit.

In like manner the Spirit compels us toward the outer edge of our spinning earth and away from the center of our own safe silos. He invites us to join him on his quest to heal a dysfunctional world.

But we tend to isolate and insulate ourselves by moving closer to the center and getting as far as we can a from world that needs a little hope. As we fight his push outward, eventually the Spirit's centrifugal force becomes imperceptible. In our cozy churches we tend to lose touch with the reality of the wider world and our sense of God's compelling call outward to reach those observing. It leaves us deaf to the voice of the Spirit, insensitive to his impetus, and feeling sick to our stomachs.

The adventure is out on the edge where he calls us to engage the world around us. Sure, it's dangerous out there and we might spin off and be injured. But if we're "sick" of our domesticated Christianity, maybe it's because we're *sequestered somewhere in the center* instead of living out on the edge where the action is, where our friendship with Jesus is best and our chances of enticing others into his friendship is maximized.

It's out there on the daring edge where we're most desperate for him to be close by. It's there we're most likely to feel his strong grasp and hear his inviting whisper to bring others onto our reeling adventure. He belays us as we careen past onlookers with outstretched arm hoping to bid everyone onto our very-merry-go-round and round and round.

It is the force of the Spirit that compels us beyond ourselves, not the force of self-recrimination and guilt. Most of us need more guilt in our lives like we need more heartburn. And we don't need another book to tell us to suck it up and force ourselves to try harder!

Do you know how many people in the world don't believe in Jesus? Me neither. Stats like that don't inspire me toward sharing my faith. They pretty much only inspire me to reach for the TV remote and a pint of Ben and Jerry's for comfort.

Christianity isn't a guilt-ridden religion; instead it's the only effective way to get rid of our guilt. Guilting ourselves into sharing our faith—or into any other spiritual practice for that matter—is not sustainable. Shouldn't our efforts to influence people toward God be more like inviting them into a cool river on a sweltering summer day?

I trust that this will be the most guilt-free, hopeful book you've read on the topic of evangelism. If it eases any unnecessary tension you have in sharing your faith I'll consider it a win.

But while sharing our faith might not always be the dessert at the end of the meal, it's certainly not Aunt Clara's dreaded spinach casserole either! Working alongside the Maker while he entices people into his embrace should be more of a dance than a dread. Ours is the matchmaker's mantra: *"I've got a Friend you should meet..."*

Sharing faith is not just for people with enough brain cells to defend the Bible's canonicity or God's Three-In-Oneness. Not only those with the audacity to stand on street corners with a megaphone can "do evangelism." Sharing God's great news is something the rest of us can do.

There's so much baggage attached to the term "evangelism" these days that I tend to replace it with alternatives such as *faith-sharing, witness-bearing, friendship-making*—even, *"gospeling"* or *"good-newsing."* Okay, so I made up the last two! Since it's my book it's my prerogative to invent words of my own, especially if I think they suggest a more holistic sense of the biblical idea of what we call "evangelism," a term that doesn't even appear in most Bible versions.

I like these alternatives because they feel more like something that has as much to do with the way we live for Jesus as what we say to people about him. Not only does "evangelism" reek of the programmatic, if not *problematic* for both the evangelizer and the evangelized, it suggests something exclusively verbal. But we're "good news" people in more ways than one. We have good news oozing out of our pores as well as passing through our lips.

So stick with me and see if you don't find something here about *faith-sharing* that you can incorporate into your own life's rhythms without having to shame yourself into it.

I suggest that a fundamental component toward a grace-filled approach to gospeling is to boil it down to *friendship*.

The Friendship Quest

> *"God has shortened the distance between us by coming here, and He has made the kingdom of heaven available in friendship form."*
> — **Carl Medearis**[1]

Before we came along, the Father, Son, and Spirit had the best, and longest standing, "Small Group" ever! Love was ubiquitous and mutually enjoyed among them. There was no rivalry or rancor in their ranks until one day they decided to expand the circle, not of divinity (that would be impossible), but of *friendship*. It wasn't that their fellowship was incomplete, but they decided to share what they had among themselves with others. Since there were no "others," they would have to "make" some friends. They had no candidates from which to choose, so they chose to create some!

They *made* one friend and then, out of the one, they made another. As idyllic as it was, it wasn't long before their new friends recklessly broke off the friendship. So, the Son was sent here on a "Friendship Quest" and paid their way back into the circle. Mission accomplished. Yet instead of remaining here to appeal to people to join the circle, he tasked his friends to do it on his behalf. His parting words, in essence, were, *Make friends with me!* "Make disciples… and I'm with you to the end of the age."[2]

If we distill down what's known as the "Great Commission" into its simplest terms, it's about *making friends with God.* You see the dual connotation, right? We begin by making friends *with him*—that is, cultivating closeness with the Creator. But soon we discover that as sweet as this friendship is, it's not all there is. As friends of God's we go about making friends with him, as in—*along with him.*

"Let's be friends," says the Creator, *"and let's go out together and make some more friends!"*

Now, doesn't that sound a little more appealing than: *"Let's go evangelize Africa!"* or *"We're going out witnessing on Friday night. Everybody come!"*?

For one thing, "Go evangelize" sounds more like an *activity* than a lifestyle. Not to mention it gives the impression that it's something we do *to* people rather than *for* them. If we don't like it done to us you can take it to the bank that they won't appreciate it being done to them.

At the same time that God befriends us he invites us into his quest for more friends. He bids us to love people for Jesus. We're his welcoming committee not so much recruiters for the Church. The similarity between inviting people into friendship and recruiting them for membership is paper-thin.

Permit a caveat or two regarding the friendship image. While it's true that *the Lord is our Friend,* it's equally true that *our Friend is the Lord*, therefore our friendship with him involves ultimate veneration and wholehearted obedience. George Buttrick calls it "a friendship held in reverence."

He's not some Cosmic Pal of ours. He's the Lord of glory, our Creator-Redeemer, who will someday sit on his seat to judge the world. Jesus fused friendship with obedience when he said that his friends do what he commands.[3] And yet, because he's such a *good Friend*, whose commands are for our *good*, it's our pleasure to obey.

I also want to make clear that the process of befriending others is not about being everybody's buddy. Our quest is not just to be the nicest, most politically correct people around. Jesus warned us that some people would take issue with our efforts to evangelize them and some would even come to hate us for it. We reach out our hand, and instead of reaching back for a boost up onto the merry-go-round, many people will resent our invitation. Rather than join our adventure they will do all they can to drag us off. The free-will rejection of some notwithstanding, we gladly take the risk and continue to extend our hand out to all.

Furthermore, I'm not a fan of either the concept of "friendship evangelism," whereby we pretend to make friends with someone just so we can evangelize them. Pretending to have an interest in someone for fifteen minutes before making your evangelistic move makes people feel manipulated. "We mustn't set these relationships up in such a way, that our efforts will be a failure if the relationships don't develop into evangelistic opportunities."[4]

The Friend Maker invites us all to join him in the quest to make friends. We bring good news, not just any good news but the news about who Jesus is, what he's done for the world, and what he's doing in us personally. One of Francis of Assisi's mottos was, "From friendship learn faith."

Not everyone is specially gifted for the good news-bearing task. We call those people "evangelists." I love evangelists. I'm not one, but I love being around them. I've known a number of evangelists over the years, those with a God-installed aptitude for attracting people to Jesus. You can't go anywhere with these flaming friendship-makers without having to peel them away from conversations with everyone they encounter along the way.

The rest of us are gifted in areas other than evangelism, yet we use those gifts to evangelize in other ways. Most of us are just plain old *witnesses* for Christ.

In some people's minds evangelism is designed exclusively for extroverts—salespersons of the month types. Which pretty much counts us ordinary people out. But you don't have to be brave to share your faith. For every one time I share my faith I wimp out at least ten times. I agree with Jim Henderson, "Boldness is overrated."[5] Even if you identify more with Woody Allen than Jason Bourne and suffer from acute "Evangelism Stress Disorder," welcome to the land of the ordinary witnesses.

If offering Jesus to people takes great boldness and super faith then just write a check for the next evangelistic event our church is putting on for Christmas and call it a day. No doubt, the cantata will be great and a good thing to invite our friends to, but writing a check and playing Mary (or Joseph as the case may be) is the very least we can do to help them find Jesus.

It might encourage you to know that Jesus didn't tell us to "go witnessing." In fact, almost every time the term "witness" is used in the New Testament (over 50 times) it appears as a noun. That is, rather than on the *act of witnessing,* God emphasizes *our identity as witnesses.* Witnesses are *what we are,* not simply something *we do.*

A witness is someone who has seen something and tells about it. "One beggar," as they say, "telling other beggars where to find bread." The pomposity of the person who recommends a pricey restaurant that he knows full well his less fortunate friends can't afford irritates me. "You should check it out," he says smugly. "The food's amazing!"

The way of the humble witness is short on sermonizing and long on confession. She shares her own spiritual poverty and invites others who are also aware of their destitution to unwrap God's grace gift.

Expertise Not Required

The first time I heard about Jesus was from a newly-saved hippie named Michael, who approached me and a friend of mine while we were sitting up in a tree smoking pot. He stood there looking up at us and told us about his radical encounter with the Lord. Though I didn't climb down out of the tree and decide to follow Jesus that day, it had an impact. I'll always be grateful for his boldness.

Shortly thereafter Jesus barreled into my life. Though I had no clue how to go about it, I was always in the hunt to share my experience with anyone with a pulse.

Beginner status and newcomer blunders notwithstanding, like anyone newly smitten, I did some of my best "witnessing" when I first fell in love with Jesus. I didn't know enough to be afraid about not knowing enough, nor had I heard enough sermons on how only bad Christians don't go witnessing with the outreach team on Saturdays.

But gradually what began as gushing about my new Best Friend, degenerated into—well—something less than enthused. When guilt, sophistication, and political correctness encroached on my joy, telling people about Jesus became less of a privilege and more of a performance.

Soon after I got saved, my church—God bless 'em—introduced us to a prefab curriculum to help us overcome our reticence to evangelize. I didn't know I was supposed to be reticent, but I figured it couldn't hurt. Looking back, I figured wrong. The manual provided us a user-friendly canned script to use. Say such and such, and if they say so and so, then you say this or that. My "witness-ees" weren't at all cooperative and would venture off the predicted course. I kept getting lost in the process and had to break out the clunky curriculum, which was armor not suited to my dimensions. I pocketed the script and proceeded to do my best with what I had to work with. Not wanting to flunk the class, I kept it quiet to my fellow "witness-ers" at the time, so I'd appreciate it if you'd keep it under your hat.

Rather than a programmatic approach, complete with conversation starters, snappy comebacks, and the latest apologetical arguments for God's realness, I'd like to invite you into a more intuitive way. This is a short book, and my name isn't Tim Keller or Ravi Zacharias, whose books on apologetics are remarkable. (See "Recommended Reading.") What I have to offer here is something other than, albeit not at all superior to, those approaches. Mine is a word, not *the last* word on sharing our faith.

"A small offering of our time, our kindness, or our attention shown toward others," says Jim Henderson, "is all Jesus needs to set up a series of divine coincidences in people's lives as he nudges them further along the path toward himself."[6] Amen!

I want to welcome you to this breathtaking journey with me and with millions of others from every time in history and every place on the planet. As we consult a particular—albeit unlikely—story from Scripture as a map, may I play tour guide for the trip?

Reaching Rahab

I got puzzled expressions when I told a few friends that I was using the Bible story of Rahab the prostitute as a framework for a book on sharing our faith, the sort of puzzlement that I have each year when trying to unravel the mysteries of an IRS tax form. "So how exactly does that story relate to evangelism?" their furrowed brows implied. I vowed that the mystery would be unfurled in the book and they'd have to buy it to understand. Now that you have—bought it, that is—I hope you'll come to understand and be inspired to love more and more people toward Jesus.

One reason I love the Bible is for its notorious cast of characters. I'd have to put the prostitute, Rahab, near the top of that list, and yet she has a prominent role in the annals of Jewish history as well as in the New Testament narrative.

Her story is recorded primarily in Joshua chapters 2 and 6. (I recommend that you read those portions before too long.) Until then here's a Reader's Digest account as a reminder:

Joshua took over from Moses as Israel's leader and led his nation into the Land of Promise. Before taking on the impenetrable city of Jericho he sent two young scouts to reconnoiter the challenges that lay ahead. The place they holed up was in the house of a prostitute named "Rahab," who hid them under the condition that they would rescue her and her family when they came back to destroy the city. After sending Jericho's king on a wild goose chase she lowered the scouts down the wall of the city by means of a red rope, the same rope she agreed to display out her window as a sign to them to save her household from their attack.

Before advancing against the city Joshua ordered his army to march around its walls for seven days in complete silence. At the end of the week they marched around the city seven times and then shouted and blew their trumpets. The massive walls crumbled and the army rushed over the rubble and routed the city.

But the scouts kept their promise and rescued Rahab and her family from the destruction, and after the battle was over, brought them in to be part of their community. Rahab went on to marry a Jewish man and had children, one of which became a progenitor of King David, and eventually an ancestor of King Jesus!

Fast forward to the New Testament where ancient Jericho's most infamous citizen is mentioned three times[7], and in each instance she comes up aces. Five short verses into the New Testament, Matthew includes her in his account of Jesus' family tree! A pagan prostitute mentioned in the same breath as Kings David and Josiah, and in the Savior's genealogy no less. She's flanked by the likes of Enoch, Moses, and Gideon in the book of Hebrews' "Faith's Hall of Fame." James highlights her as one whose good works authenticate her as a believer of the same spiritual stripe as Abraham. Pretty impressive cred I say.

I concede that this is not your stock story from which to draw inspiration for sharing faith with not-yet-believers. In fact, I've never heard anyone teach on that topic from it. The story is typically told with a focus on the miraculous felling of Jericho's walls and God's *conquest* over his enemies. But there's something else that I see folded into the narrative, having to do with his *quest* for friends. We preachers usually use the story to sermonize about God's power to judge, not his grace to save. But let's remember that God made those impenetrable walls fall flat not just to let the Israelites *in,* but also to let one prostitute and her family *out!*

So I ask you to indulge me and see if you don't pick up the least little connection between this story and God's passionate pursuit of people and how we might join him in his pursuit.

After all, the name "Joshua" is the Hebrew equivalent of "Jesus." Both mean *Savior.* Could there be an implied correspondence between Jesus commissioning his disciples to go out in pairs to bring people to him, and Joshua sending his two scouts out to rescue Rahab and bring her and her family back to him?

If you think about it, if Joshua's scouts had done a door-to-door poll of who might become a believer in the God of the Jews, I'm sure Rahab would've been way down the list of candidates.

She fit in the category of *the least likely* in Jericho to be a follower of Yahweh.

However, I meet *"Rahabs"* in my city (San Francisco) all the time, people that—like the prostituted woman in the Bible story—are severely *broken,* yet positively *beloved* by God. Like her, many of them contain a *spacious spirit* (Rahab means "spacious"), yet you wouldn't know it for the walls behind which they hide.

Rahabs are broken women and men who may or may not make their living from other people's brokenness, and yet they have something inside that points them in the general direction of the Repairer of the Broken. They live lost lives, and yet clearly possess an internal *GPS (God Positioning System)* that shows them where they are now and how to get where they were made to go.

Twisted and confused by their inherent bent toward rebellion, humans are at the same time stamped by God as divine image bearers, his one-off work of art. To focus on one or the other exclusively either demonizes or deifies them. They're neither demons nor divine, but lost sons and daughters—seldom as bad as they could be, but never enough good to not need a Savior.

Jesus prioritized the *Rahabs* of his day, the most defective individuals in Israel: the five-time divorcée from Samaria, the Canaanite widow, blind Bartimaeus, Zacchaeus the extortionist, the thankful leper, and the demonized Gadarene to name a few. He gravitated to people who needed him most, ones whose hearts were primed for his intervention. Rahab, a woman of the night and believer in Canaanite idols, was just such a person.

For my money the most fascinating part of the narrative is that before the two scouts even show up at her door, Rahab is aware of who God is. And she is quite willing, when given the chance, to reach out to him for help. Her city was about to be decimated. Everyone in Jericho had heard reports about God drowning Pharaoh's army in the Red Sea and leading his people into successful campaigns against their enemies. They are terrified by what was coming, but one person—the least likely of their number—goes out of her way to escape her doom.

How fortuitous that the two scouts who are reconnoitering the impermeable city of Jericho would come to *her* house—her house of ill repute. Of all people, God reaches out to her, and she reaches back.

Instead of checking into the local Motel 6 where they'd stand out, they go to a brothel where they could blend in. I know it looks bad on paper, but I'm pretty sure they weren't there as patrons. If you think about it, it makes perfect sense that they'd go to her house where there would be a lot of men traipsing in and out of her door. The spies go where no one would notice them, and anyone who did would be less likely to report it. What happens at Rahab's stays at Rahab's! Sound strategy notwithstanding, the word did get out and the king's men came looking for them.

There was an ominous buzz throughout the whole city about the doom that was to come. Their impenetrable walls had shielded them from countless assaults in the past, but the storm that was gathering outside brought with it a higher threat level than ever before. You can almost hear their conversations: *These Jews have a big bad god on their side. He divides seas and fights alongside his armies. We're in trouble!*

But Rahab has something more going on inside of her. Though she is as frightened as anyone, she intuits a hint of hope for escape. She couldn't quite pin it down, but something inside said, *"You don't have to die today!"*

When the two scouts come to her door, her heart leaps. Might this be what she had been hoping in her hoper all along? She takes the "evangelists" in, hides them, and makes up a story of their whereabouts. Before sending them on their way she seizes the opportunity and pleads for mercy for her and her whole family. She doesn't wait for them to proffer any sort of deal for her salvation; she speaks up first and they consent—with conditions. She fulfills her part of the bargain and they keep their promise. When the walls come tumbling down she and her whole family are saved!

My inquiry into Rahab's "conversion" has given me a new notion on shattered souls, some new ways to pray for them, and a greater expectation of bringing them into friendship with Jesus. Based on this story I'd like to offer some Friendship Quest advice that I hope you'll find helpful.

Use us, Lord, to reach Rahabs!

PART ONE

A Supernaturally Installed Wonder

> *"There is a universal urge to transcend—a basic capacity to experience the sacred."*
> — Clark Pinnock[8]

> *"I know that the LORD has given you this land and that a great fear of you has fallen on us, so that all who live in this country are melting in fear because of you. We have heard how the LORD dried up the water of the Red Sea for you . . . When we heard of it, our hearts melted in fear and everyone's courage failed because of you, for the LORD your God is God in heaven above and on the earth below."*
> — Joshua 2:9-11

We all know people who, like Rahab, have a supernaturally installed respect for God. Though they might be squandering their lives at the moment, it's obvious that they have "eternity in their heart."[9] Their respect for the deity doesn't necessarily mean they know him personally or love him in their hearts yet, but it is a huge step in the right direction.

Rahab indicates that many of her fellow Jerichoans have a fear akin to hers: "Great fear has fallen on *us... all* who live in this country are melting in fear... *everyone's* courage failed because of you..."[10] Hyperbole notwithstanding, there were a lot of people in the city that were more than a little nervous about the god of those crazy Jews who were camped on the other side of the river!

But Rahab's outlook went beyond fear of death. Her heart was open to hope. Her name actually means "spacious" or roomy. Her spirit had the bandwidth for a supernaturally installed wonder about her Creator. Like Cornelius the centurion or Zacchaeus the tax collector, Rahab the prostitute had plenty of free space on her *heart drive* for the truth about the one true God.

You'll notice that each time she referred to God she called him by the name that only the Jews used: "Yahweh." (Whenever you see "LORD" in all caps, it's a translation of that special name for the God of the Jews.) They had all heard stories of the conquests of this God of the Hebrews, and at least one person believed what she'd heard.

She had no Bibles on her nightstand or Baptists in her neighborhood. There were no preachers on TV or people on street corners handing out tracts and yet when the scouts showed up at her door she was already a "believer" of sorts. Rahab knew that she and her fellow citizens were in danger of being on the wrong side when disaster arrived and yet she possessed hope—albeit a faint hope—for a way of escape.

The stories of God's supernatural interventions have a power to them. They certainly factored heavily into Rahab's "pre-faith." Someone had seen what God did at the Red Sea and they told someone who told someone else, and so on, till the accounts arrived in Jericho and filtered through the population.

The witnesses, though most likely unaware of what they set in motion, did what witnesses do. They witnessed! They told the story.

They witnessed by hearing about or seeing the Jews crossing the Red Sea and they bore witness of what they saw. That's what witnesses do. They experience something and they tell about it. Simple as that.

The takeaway here is: If you've seen God in something, tell the story! Your God-sighting stories have an impact on others. Tell the stories of whatever Red Seas he's parted for you. Those you tell may or may not rush directly into Jesus' arms. It might take some time for them to get around to it. But in the meantime they might pass the story on to someone whose spirit is ready, which is what happened to Rahab. You just never know the circuitous path your story will travel. But it won't travel anywhere if you don't tell it.

Not long ago I experienced the power of story while talking with "Ken," a guy who has been living in Golden Gate Park for a number of years. This friend of mine is no newcomer to spiritual themes. You might think of him as a fan of philosophy and a banterer about religions of all sizes and shapes. Our first interaction bogged down, as my argument was too heavily weighted on propositional truth and not enough on my own story about how Jesus has worked in my life. When I changed my route and started sharing some of my own God-sighting stories, his demeanor shifted and he put his spiritualistic spiel on pause long enough to unlatch one of the many deadbolts on his heart's door.

Like the citizens of Jericho, for protection from pain, people wall themselves in. Problem is, the same barriers that safeguard them from others also serve to barricade them against the truth about the Lover of their soul. Using logic to persuade them to open the gate is usually about as effective as the Jews trying to argue the Jerichoans into letting them in.

The more direct and logical approach to good news telling tends to work a little better after a level of trust has been established by the power of story and they've cracked open the door a bit.

Rahab's heart must have sung when the scouts rang her doorbell that day. Their appearance fanned her spark of faith into flame. Divine appointments like these are key to God's rescue operations.

I wish I had a nickel for every time I've seen that the Spirit has clearly been at work in someone's heart ahead of my meager efforts to show up and share with them about Jesus. The grace-clues that the Spirit concocted converged to ready Rahab for rescue remind me of Philip's arrival at the precise moment the Ethiopian was charoting by, reading one of the Bible's profoundest prophecies of Jesus' crucifixion (Isaiah 53). That's what I call a divine appointment!

Notice Rahab's "statement of faith":

"The LORD your God is God in heaven above and on the earth below..."

Prostituted idolater notwithstanding, Rahab has a pretty good idea of who God is. She had been raised to worship other deities and maybe still has an emotional attachment to them, but somehow she knows that the God of the Jews has more—a bunch more— clout than her own gods.

> *Your God is above, below, and beyond our gods; so I'm looking for a little help here. Maybe you could put in a good word to him for me before he takes over our city!*

Surely this is a woman with a supernaturally installed sense of wonder.

God, in his passionate pursuit of people, is way out ahead of us. He's always first on the scene. He's on a friendship-making frenzy, instilling seeds of purpose in people's hearts. There's nowhere we can go that he hasn't already been, preparing people's hearts to take hold of his love.

Over the years I've been taken by surprise by thousands of divine appointments with Rahab-like "closet pre-Christians" who secretly harbor a hope of Someone watching and caring. I confess that I've squandered way too many of these eternally ordained opportunities out of fear, busyness, or a sluggish attention to the Spirit. But there's nothing like being part of a divine setup designed to coax people out of their locked rooms and into his loving arms.

Now, when I look at a person, instead of measuring how far they are from God, I try to discern what the Spirit is doing in them to bring them close. What sort of wonder has already been supernaturally installed in them?

"Speak to the spark!" That's what I often tell people who are learning how to offer Jesus to people. Speak to the spark inside them, with which they were born. It's the precursor to the flame that Jesus wants to ignite inside them. That spark consists of the same thing that is ablaze inside you. You're acquainted with it, so speak to it, blow on it, and see what happens!

All Jerichoans had Yahweh and the storm he was bringing on their minds. The Spirit had, for some time, been passionately pursuing their entire citizenry. He inserted himself into their consciences through the stories they'd heard. Rahab and her family may have been the only ones who escaped the judgment, but the Spirit had been revealing himself to her neighbors for generations. Since it's in his nature to chase after people to befriend them, it's natural to presume that he would do all he could to warn everyone of the judgment to come. He has no desire for anyone to perish but for everyone to accept his invitation to friendship.[11]

Someone once envisioned a mythical encounter between the heavenly gate-keeper, Peter and the Apostle Paul. Peter had noticed that there were more souls inside the pearly gates than were accounted for in the books. Paul explained that Jesus was sneaking them over the wall when Peter wasn't looking!

Like I said, this is mythical, but it's not entirely uncharacteristic of a God driven to passionately pursue people wherever they are. Let's unpack a few of the schemes he employed to charm Rahab and her family into friendship with him.

God's Passionate Pursuit of People

> *"Reality is that which, when you stop
> believing in it, doesn't go away."*
> — Philip K. Dick

I thought I had found Jesus until I realized he found me. He'd been following me around all my life when I finally looked over my shoulder and noticed him. The day I asked Jesus to save me, it wasn't because the preacher said I should. I was beckoned.

If we look closely at the backstory of our friend Rahab, she too was beckoned. Her "conversion" didn't happen in a vacuum. The Spirit actively planted invitations in and around her in preparation for her to ultimately encounter Yahweh.

God is not sitting on his hands, waiting for people to discover him. As the ultimate missionary, he passionately pursues people and circulates invitations to friendship in every possible place. He's *patient* for those he loves to bow the knee, but he's not at all *passive* about it. He's obsessed with bringing his children back home.

The idea that God sits back and hopes that people will take advantage of his invitation to friendship is unworthy of him. He's as relentless in his quest for people to enjoy his redemption as he was eager to send his redeeming Son in the first place. I suggest that it is as difficult to run away from God as it is to run away from gravity. He keeps pulling us back to him.

He's wrapped in mystery and often "hides in darkness," yet he is a God whose personality it is to reveal himself to the people. His mercy is wide, his love is stubborn, and his hospitality is prodigal. He's determined to be known and to be enjoyed.

He leaves clues all over the place about his power and personality, which *"go out into all the earth, their words to the ends of the world."*[12]

Little Bo-Peep has lost her sheep
And doesn't know where to find them
Leave them alone and they will come home
Wagging their tails behind them.

I don't know who this girl is, but I don't think she knows much about sheep. Leaving them alone isn't the best strategy. They don't usually find their way home on their own. Someone has to go get them. When he loses one, Jesus "leaves the ninety-nine" and goes after it. And he drafts us to join him in the rescue.

If you watch Alfred Hitchcock films closely, you'll be able to spot him at least in one obscure scene. He may show up in a crowded restaurant or a bus station, but if you look for him, you'll see that he always makes a cameo appearance.

For the sake of those he loves, the Creator also appears in scores of covert "God sightings." As he did with Rahab, he passes through all our lives in many ways and at many times, in hopes that we'll freeze the frame and take notice.

When we paused long enough to notice him amidst the crowd of "extras" we became "witnesses." We *witnessed* him popping in and out of our stories and decided to jump into his storyline. From there we began inviting others into the narrative. We're both *witnesses of him* and *witnesses for him.*

As with Joshua's scouts' interaction with Rahab, our *witness for him* is entirely collaborative. We're not independent contractors. We're "God's co-workers."[13] (It's a *Great* Commission because a *Great* God concocted it. And it's a Great *Co-mission* because he invited us to do it along with him.)

Jesus said, "Take my yoke upon you and learn from me, for I am gentle and humble in heart, and you will find rest for your souls. For my yoke is easy and my burden is light."[14]

Our job is not to shoulder the weight of the world's lost souls. It's *his* yoke, not ours. He supplies all the pulling power, so when we "co-operate"—collaborate—with him, we find that the burden of the work is his. His yoke is built for two necks—his and ours! Best I can tell, yokes make for some pretty close quarters, the proximity of which makes it easier for his compassionate heart to rub off onto ours and for him to whisper his directives into our ears. Intimacy with Jesus inspires and empowers ministry for Jesus. When we hear his whisper and walk in step with him, he does the heavy lifting!

God generously distributes friendship invitations. Along with Rahab, we have accounts of the Passionate Pursuer pursuing other off-the-beaten-trail non-Hebrew people, such as Job the sufferer[15], Balaam the pagan prophet[16], Abimelech the Gentile king[17], the Magi from the East[18], Cornelius the Centurion[19] and many more.

Jesus tells us that God, the Shepherd, goes after the one lost sheep with such ferocity that he momentarily leaves the ninety-nine to fend for themselves.[20] John describes Jesus as "the true light that gives light to everyone coming into the world."[21] Jesus said that the Father is "always at work"[22] and that he too works to "draw all people" to himself[23]. Furthermore, he said that the Spirit speaks to people in the world about "sin, righteousness, and judgment."[24] Paul also makes the point that God "testifies" by showing kindness to people in giving them rain and food.[25]

We're told in the Bible's final chapter that the Spirit invites the "thirsty" to come and "take the free gift of the water of life" and that the Bride (us!) join him in his invitation[26].

The grand story of the Maker's quest for friends begins in a garden wherein we disregarded his ruling and tasted the illicit fruit. True to his threat, through the sadness, he removed us from the verdant paradise, locked the gate, and posted a guard.

But he loved us far too much to bar us in perpetuity. So, the Father, Son, and Spirit convened to devise a way to redeem and return us to friendship forever.

Willing to go to any length to bring us back, their generous plan came at a dreadful price. The Son would gladly take our guilty place, be convicted of our crimes, and suffer banishment from Trinitarian fellowship on our behalf.

Though Jesus paid the outrageous ransom price, still many refuse to return to where we belong. So, part of the plan is to allure us all, to entice us back home. The Spirit would traverse the globe with a huge stash of friendship invitations and scatter them liberally in every place that we expelled souls live. His love is extravagant and his passion profuse to propagate his plea in every place possible.

Not content to do it alone, he invites us to collaborate in his grace errand to reach others with the offer of friendship. "Let's go together," he says, "and invite people to come home!" We partner with the Creator to scatter invitations throughout the world to entice them back to him—and to us.

He includes us in the mission, not because he needs our help, but in order to give us the privilege of partnering with him, which is why we call it a "co-mission," a mission we do in tandem with him.

Because the Spirit's relentless efforts go a long way to bring people home, in some cases what we call "evangelism" is little more than a simple confirmation of what he has already put in their heart, whether they know it or not. Some people, as in the case of Rahab, are already mulling over an RSVP to his invitation. All they need is someone to take them by the hand and bring them home.

Rahab, a collector of divine invitations, is a vivid example of such a person. By the time Joshua's scouts arrived at her door, she was already half way to friendship with Yahweh.

She Sees God in Creation

> *"The heavens declare the glory of God; the skies proclaim the work of his hands. Day after day they pour forth speech; night after night they reveal knowledge. There is no speech or language where their voice is not heard. Their voice goes out into all the earth, their words to the ends of the world."*
> — **Psalm 19:1-4**

The Creator made his world with such wonder that clues about him abound at Rahab's every glance. When she looked up there was no denying that there is a power, and maybe even a Person behind the power, greater than her.

Sunflowers, the human brain, humming birds, and just enough gravity to keep us from floating away yet not so much as to flatten us like crêpes! When she observed the night sky she would be hard pressed to muster the faith to conclude that we just evolved this way without the supervision of a superior intelligence.

The stars speak every language, even "Jerichoan." The Spirit places tiny public address systems at sunrises, waterfalls, and baby smiles. These whispered God's friendship invitation in Rahab's native tongue. Something inside her said, "Yes, I'm here…"

It appears that her fellow citizens were not as receptive to the voice in the skies. Centuries later Paul says that through his creation *"God's invisible qualities—his eternal power and divine nature—have been clearly seen, being understood from what has been made, so that people are without excuse."*[27] Some people muster the will to believe that this world all just happened without a Designer.

Others choose to enjoy the *created* and avoid its *Creator,* or they identify creation *with* the Creator as though they're one and the same. We should always be thankful *for* trees, mountains, and seascapes, but never be thankful *to* them.

From Seagulls to stars, from a grain of sand to a snow-capped peak, each created thing contains a unique footprint of God's, whose memo is, *"Go ahead and enjoy. Oh, and by the way, I love you!"*

I honestly think that it takes more work to miss the Maker than it does to find him. He gives *light* to everyone[28], and though we can always lower the blinds and shut the light out[29], doing so is not only ill-advised, it actually takes more effort than to simply let it in. Rahab left the blinds open.

I almost never encounter a true atheist, someone who claims to *know* there is no God. "Agnostics," on the other hand, abound, people who admit they don't know. But there's no one-size-fits-all agnostic. They come in different sizes and shapes.

When I inquired which brand of agnostic "Kelly" was she confessed that she was unaware of more than one. "Well," I said, "there's the kind that say, 'I don't know if there is a God but am open to suggestion.' Then there's the one who claims, 'I don't know, you don't know, nobody can know!'" I was glad when she espoused affiliation with the first brand. It's easier to appeal to someone who is open to appeal.

I resisted the temptation to whip out my handy-dandy evidences for God. In hopes that she'd recognize some of her own, I just told her the ways I see and appreciate the artistry of the Creator in snowfall, tropical fish, and the amazing human brain. She didn't come right out and admit it but her eyes said she was intrigued. Maybe she's one inch closer to home.

When Rahab gazed up after dark there's no doubt that she saw the wonder and heard the "voice" bidding her toward his kingdom of light. Who's to know but that her revelation of God may have equaled, or even surpassed, that of the scouts!

But wait. There's more…

She Sees God in Her Conscience

> *"(Indeed, when Gentiles, who do not have the law, do by nature things required by the law, they are a law for themselves, even though they do not have the law. They show that the requirements of the law are written on their hearts, their consciences also bearing witness, and their thoughts sometimes accusing them and at other times even defending them.) This will take place on the day when God judges people's secrets through Jesus Christ, as my gospel declares."*
> — **Romans 2:14-16**

God coyly installs invitations inside every person in the form of a conscience. If people have *"the requirements of the law are written on their hearts,"* Someone must have done the writing! Right?

It's not a perfect rule of thumb because it can be skewed or silenced by relentless inattention. But when it's in good working order, the conscience points directly to the One who installed it.

I have no doubt that in the quiet of her heart Rahab knew that her trade corroded her soul and that Someone had something more for her than this. When she looked inside she saw Someone looking out.

"*Conscience,*" said C.S. Lewis *"is the inner voice that warns us that somebody's watching."*[30] It's sort of a *compass* that God surgically implanted in each of us at birth that tells us if we're going the right direction or not. *"You find out more about God from the Moral Law (conscience) than from the universe (creation); just as you find out more about a man by listening to his conversation than by looking at a house he built."*

My friend Dan told me his view of the role of the conscience.

God turns on his light, and from the great distance between him and us the beam seems like a speck, as does a star from its position light years away. If we take a step toward him—instead of further away—he takes one toward us, and the speck appears larger than before. It seems to increase in size and lumens as we move closer to its source until finally, what seemed like a pinpoint beam, now directly in front of us, is a blazing sun. What was once tiny in the distance now fills our entire line of sight. Conversely, if we move away from the light or attempt to block it out, it becomes smaller and smaller until it finally disappears altogether.

God does all he can to get the beam to find its way around our attempts to quash it. He directs his beam from another angle, and then another, and still another until finally we either surrender to him or reject him from every direction. He's relentless like that, I believe, until our last breath.

Before the scouts rang her doorbell, Rahab had *inside information* about Yahweh. At the same time creation told her he was great her conscience asserted his moral requirements.

Paul said, "Every matter must be established by the testimony of two or three witnesses."[31] In addition to the witness of creation and conscience, Rahab and her neighbors saw at least an oblique semblance of the divine in *human culture*.

She Sees God in Her Culture

> "Greece, Egypt, ancient India, the beauty of the world, the pure and authentic reflection of this beauty in art and science...these things have done as much as the visibly Christian ones to deliver me into Christ's hands as his captive."
> — SIMONE WEIL

Creation *in front of Rahab*, conscience *inside her*, and her culture *all around her* allured her to friendship with her Maker. Evidently, God really wants to be known! He surrounds us inside and out with traces of revelation. He expresses his creativity through the creativity of his created.

When I hear Santana play the guitar, gaze at a painting by Rembrandt, or read the novels of Twain, something inside me is warmed. I feel it when I sing our national anthem, see people in love walking down the street hand in hand, or watch Mexican folkloric dances.

When she sat at a meal with her family celebrating their age-old customs of one thing or another, in the closeness and camaraderie, Rahab undoubtedly heard a faint whisper, "This warmth you're feeling is part of a larger story you're in…"

Through what he made *directly* in creation, God leaves clues about his *power*. But he doesn't stop there. He continues to cultivate in us an awareness of his *person* through the things he creates *indirectly*, i.e. through people as demonstrated in human culture—art, community, science, traditions, mores, and more. "The human race as a whole has the image of God in a collective sense—so that the rich diversity of cultures on the face of the earth shows forth the splendor of God in a way that no individual or group does alone," says Richard Mouw.[32]

Albeit quite different from ours, the culture of Jericho had its own share of evidence of the divine. God's invitations find their way into all forms of human civilization. Someone defined the term "culture" as "the cultivation of the soul." We can see how the Creator leaves snapshots of himself in our cultures in order to "cultivate our soul," and to dispose that soul toward himself.

The Trinity convened and said, *"Let us make man in our image, after our likeness…"* From eternity past they lived in perfect and unbroken community. Part of what it means to be made in God's image is our human inclination for living in relationship and community. Human bonds are clues that we're made in the likeness of a relational God. Our Maker loves and yearns to be loved, and installed the relational code in our DNA. Rahab's insistence to include her family along with her in the rescue is evidence of that.

Even when a society fails, when it implodes on itself by its anti-God mores, God takes advantage of it by offering an alternative. We learn by negative examples as well as by positive. God uses instances of botched society—the cumulative failure of its members—to beckon people to himself. People who are frustrated by the failure of their society may be thus incited toward his superlative society.

Prior to experiencing the benefit of a human witness, Rahab seemed to have a fairly honed sense of what God is like. Undoubtedly, there were elements in her culture that pointed her toward Yahweh. Yet much of what we know of pagan culture in her day would lead us to believe that much of her culture directed her so diametrically opposite of Paradise that it drove her to run to Yahweh for a better way.

His message to Jericho would likely be more of one by contrast, *"Obviously, what you're doing is not functional, so how about taking a chance at a better way—my way!"* The society that rejects him and suffers the consequences is one way he entices people toward the better society.

Rahab, for one, took that message to heart and ran to God and to his people for that better way.

She Sees God in Her Crises

> *"God whispers to us in our pleasures, speaks in our consciences, but shouts in our pains. Pain is God's megaphone to rouse a deaf world."*
> — **C.S. Lewis**[33]

Suffering has a way of humbling us, forcing us to look up. Our *emergencies* are some of God's best *opportunities* to get our attention. Pain of all types slows us down enough to notice his invitations to friendship.

Jericho's crisis was one of life and death. I have no doubt that the Spirit went through every neighborhood pleading with the terrified citizens as they peered over the edge of their ramparts at the Hebrews marching around their city in silence. I imagine him giving each person every chance to choose life instead of death.

Rahab made the right choice, as did my friend "Samantha." She grew up with two alcoholic parents, who left her and her young siblings unsupervised for days at a time. On a number of nights she had to drag them out of the bar, take them home, and put them to bed. The only solace that Samantha found was in the nearby Catholic Church where she huddled in the silence alone and felt the presence of Jesus. He was "close" to that brokenhearted little girl day after day. Today, after many years of *time off for bad behavior,* she's a licensed minister in her church, telling her story to other fearful and forlorn souls.

Another Rahab-like friend of mine, "Ken" met Jesus in the middle of a drug overdose. Any one of the lethal three street drugs he took that night would have stopped his heart; the combination of the three was a sure death sentence. I'd say that qualifies as a crisis! In the hospital he flat-lined when Jesus appeared to him, urged him to follow him, and breathed life back into his lungs. He's now a house church pastor and leads a discipleship house for men coming out of prison or off the street.

Sometimes, without changing the circumstances, the Father sits with an abandoned child assuring her with his sweet presence. Other times he intervenes in a not-yet-Christian's crisis and transforms the circumstances in order to entice him or her toward him. Either way, he advances his friendship-making agenda.

About gospeling and the ultimate crisis

I have no doubt that the first thought on Rahab's mind was how to *get out* of Jericho before it was annihilated. However I imagine the second item on her agenda would've been, "Then where do we go?" Evidently, as an alternative, the men with whom she was negotiating promised her and her family a secure place in their community[34]. The prospect of knowing the God of the Hebrews and joining their community would have more than sweetened the deal.

Everyone, whether they know it or not, face the ultimate crisis about where they'll go when they die. Our gospel tells us that Jesus is the only One who can rescue us from the bad place and take us to *the good place.*

All humans face *the ultimate crisis*—that of leaving this life without a relationship with our Maker. I believe that real people will stand before a real God to be judged. I have seen some people run to Jesus primarily to avoid hell, but since most postmodern people have little sense of the eternal, it's not that common.

I'm aware that the gospels record more of Jesus' preaching about hell than about heaven, but I would point out that his Jewish audiences were already familiar with the threat of judgment and so to them it would be nothing meaningless or absurd. On the other hand, in their conversations and sermons in the book of Acts, the apostles seldom referred to judgment, especially when speaking to a Gentile audience.

In his very first public sermon, Jesus turned to Isaiah 61 in order to spell out his mission statement—*to preach to the poor, free prisoners, heal the blind, set oppressed people free, and proclaim the favor of the Lord.* But then he stopped short of Isaiah's very next phrase, "to proclaim the day of God's vengeance." He omitted the part about judgment. Why?

I suppose it was because judgment wasn't part of his core message. He fearlessly warned people about judgment at times, but it wasn't his primary calling. I doubt that anyone would accuse him of being tentative or politically correct. He just knew when to break out his hell warnings and when not to. It was the Lord's "favor" that he favored in his preaching. I can't improve on that in my own good news telling.

I'm not saying that we should never talk to people about the fearful prospect of eternity apart from God. I'm just saying that sharing the hope of a better future may be a more effective way to nudge people toward Jesus than threatening them with the prospect of judgment. Fear of hell may work for some, but the message of hope of heaven, to say nothing of a better future here on earth, is more likely to connect to the hearts of most postmodern people.

Don't be afraid to warn people about standing before God, but wisely pick your spots. Jonathan Edwards' sermon, "Sinners in the Hands of an Angry God" was biblical and effective in his day and there are some contexts in which we will be prompted by the Spirit to issue similar warnings to our friends. But, in my opinion, generally speaking, rather than emphasizing avoiding hell, a more effective way in these days of skepticism about religion is to coax them toward heaven.

To be honest, I seldom try to scare people with hell or entice them with heaven. I simply offer them Jesus. I want them to fall in love with him, not just use him to avoid the one place in favor of the other. He said he was "the way" to the Father, not just the way to get to heaven. Our gospel is Jesus.

Hence, Rahab realized that Yahweh had placed his invitations in her life's crises. Now I propose that God also inserted invitations in her religion.

She Sees God in Her Creed

> *"God sent the human race what I call good dreams: I mean those queer (strange) stories scattered through all the heathen religions about a god who dies and comes to life again and, by his death, has somehow given new life to men."*
> — **C.S. Lewis**[35]

Rahab and her fellow citizens had a religion. Whatever form it took, whatever theological flaws it contained, their creed gave them at least an oblique concept of the divine. Even in her pagan religious customs I have no doubt that she "heard" the Spirit's serenade.

Their defective theology notwithstanding, its redeeming qualities might well have paved their way to the way to the true God. (Please note my intentional phrasing, "paved their way to the way to God," as opposed to their religion being a way that would get them directly to God.)

The God who journeys to the ends of the earth to make himself known happily ventured even into the realm of Rahab's flawed religion.

I'm sure that the Spirit had tossed thousands of friendship invitations over Jericho's wall and that some of them landed in their religious creed. These must have facilitated Rahab's way to faith in the God of the Jews. They acted as a preamble to the rest of the truth about him. I have no doubt that over time, in favor of what she discovered about Yahweh, she rejected the false ideas of her former religion.

Even in largely false religious systems, there exists some redemptive quality. Notice I didn't say, "redeeming," which would imply that people can be redeemed through a defective dogma, apart from Jesus.

"'Redemptive' in this context," says Don Richardson in his seminal book, *Eternity in their Hearts*, "means 'contributing to the redemption of people, but not culminating in it.' Redemptive lore contributes to the redemption of a people solely by facilitating their understanding of what redemption means. Their own lore caused the Mbaka people (an African tribe that were eventually brought to Christ through missionary efforts) to see the gospel as something to be treasured, not as something imposed arbitrarily by a foreigner."[36]

An African Christian leader told what it had been like for him to turn away from animistic religion to embrace Christ. "There were many things in my tribe's religious stories that prepared me for the gospel. When I first heard the story of Jesus, it did not strike me as a completely new and strange thing. What I said to myself was, 'Aha! So that is the answer!'"[37]

Is Jesus the only way to God? A definite yes! But there's a difference between different ways to God and different ways God uses to get people *to the way.*

God is willing to travel any road to find people who haven't yet found the way. He stubbornly hunts for the hearts of people and even plants his invitations in less than perfect *religious soils.*

Because he cares about the billions of Muslims, Hindus, and Buddhists of the world, he slips clues about himself in their systems of worship. Yes, Jesus is the only *non-stop flight* to the Father; that much is clear (John 14:6; Acts 4:12; 1 Timothy 2:5).[38] But the Spirit leaves invitations on other flights and in other airports to encourage travellers to eventually board the plane that will take them all the way to God.

The pagan faith of the Jerichoans was a *repository* of an unknown concentration of truth. No doubt it contained *truths* but not *The Truth.* God's stubborn love compels him to use whatever means he can in order to gain entrance into the starving spirits of open-hearted followers of other religions.

Most, if not all, faiths have one concentration of truth or another within its dogma, but let's be clear, the Mother Lode is in Jesus! He's the end of all things and the beginning of all things. Everything that's savingly true leads back to him[39].

Jesus announced himself as the light of the world. Light is made up of the sum total of the colors of the spectrum. "Jesus as light gathers up the different colored truths and goodness of all who have gone before. Each one can find his distinctive national or religious color in Christ. But we do not want colors we want light. Christ is the sum-total of the colors, but he is more. He is light itself."[40]

Yet the Spirit is anything but stingy with solicitations. His mailbag overflows as he distributes clues of the Father's love, whose default is to *include* rather than *exclude* people from his family. Jesus overpaid for as many orphans as would come home with him. And he doesn't care which orphanage in which he finds them! Conveying a welcome as wide as his should be our ambition.

I'd like to think that if I were sharing my faith with Rahab, instead of merely identifying what was wrong with her ideas, I would celebrate what was true in her theology and build on that. I would acknowledge that the Spirit had been to Jericho sprinkling divine realities ahead of me and then hopefully collaborate with him to beckon her and her townspeople toward Jesus.

I'll talk some more about how to share Jesus with people of other faiths in the chapter called, "The Jesus Bus."

Now finally, and hopefully most fully, the Sower sows seeds through *Christians*.

Enter – A Pair of "Witnesses"

> *"A candle loses nothing by lighting another candle."*

As is his habit, the Spirit had already been enticing the Jerichoans well before Joshua's scouts turned up. It could be said that Rahab and her neighbors were "pre-evangelized" by what they had seen and heard *in Creation, in Conscience, in Culture, in Crises,* and even in aspects of their *Creed.*

But that is not to say that God has no place in his friendship-making project for *Christians.* On the contrary, our celebration of the influence of the Spirit's invitations in advance of us notwithstanding, we're an indispensible component in his plan in nudging people toward repentance and faith. He employs both inanimate and animate forms of persuasion—the former prepares the way for the latter, the latter (us) being his ace in the hole. People come to know God through relationship with another person who knows God.

Joshua's two scouts weren't "Christians" in the classic sense and it's not like they were going door to door handing out Yahweh tracts. But if you try, you might be able to imagine their interaction with Rahab as "witnessing." Their appearance confirmed the ways that the Spirit had already been saying to her. The things she'd seen *above* her, *inside* her, *around* her, *below* her, and *beyond* her readied her for contact with the two ambassadors from God's camp. She already possessed a measure of revelation of God's personality and power, and as a result, was ready to hear the message of rescue.

The spies were Jewish and Rahab was not. They somehow bridged the breach between cultures, languages, and religious dogmas. "I entered their world," says Paul, "and tried to experience things from their point of view. I've become just about every sort of servant there is in my attempts to lead those I meet into a God-saved life."[41]

God prepares people ahead of us, so that when we come to clarify the clues he's sown in and around them there's something to which our message may attach. It's virtually impossible for us to engage with someone with whom the Spirit has not already been working in some way. As we go around inviting people to the party we may rest assured that he has already filled their pockets with invitations. Pretty exciting! Right?

As God's "co-workers" when we call people to come to Jesus we're joining in the Spirit's serenade: *"The Spirit and the Bride say come..."*[42]

Some call it *"prevenient grace,"* others use the phrase *"common grace"* to describe what the Spirit does to prepare people to hear about his *"saving grace."* Whatever you want to call it, the Spirit uses anything he chooses to sing his "Come to Jesus!" song, and then invites us to harmonize with him!

We might think of common grace as a "frontage road" from whence people can see the freeway through the chain link fence. We offer an onramp for them to use to jump on the "free-way" (cheesy pun intended) of salvation.⁴³

That he does all the preparatory work doesn't mean that we are somehow expendable. Not at all. In his effort to bring spiritual orphans home he includes us. He doesn't need our help, yet he's chosen to involve us in his great people-loving, kingdom-building, friendship-making project. Partners with the Almighty in his quest to charm people into his family! What could be better?

Probably more often than we realize, our role is to introduce people to the God they already believe in, but don't know much about. Though their knowledge of him is obscured with errors, we come in to "show and tell" what he's actually like—as best we can, anyway.

"Always be prepared," says Peter, *"to give an answer to everyone who asks you to give the reason for the hope that you have."*⁴⁴ In a world bereft of it, humans crave hope. When they actually see in us hope incarnate they might just ask us to give a reason for it.

Rahab's heart skipped a beat when Joshua's scouts arrived at her house as ambassadors of hope. Her revelation of Yahweh was incomplete. As many do, she hoped there was hope to be had, so she tapped into theirs.

People's pockets bulge with friendship invitations, clues of God's love. Either they haven't noticed them or they don't know what to do with them. It's our privilege to clarify the cache of clues that they've unconsciously collected over time. I've had conversations similar to this:

> *You know you're invited, right? God wants you as his friend.*
>
> *I don't know what you're talking about. I have no such invitation.*
>
> *That can't be true. I know he invites everyone to his party and he wouldn't leave you out. Check your pockets again.*
>
> *Okay, I found a so-called "invitation," but what's it mean? Invitation to what, to whom?*

Now we're off to the races!

We'll Take That "To Go"

"Evangelism is bringing a person one step closer to Christ."

Knowing this about God that he "passionately pursues people" helps me how?

It helps me not be in such a rush.

When I was in college I worked at UPS unloading trucks. We usually worked in pairs hoisting packages onto a conveyor belt. It wasn't long before my reputation as an annoying Christian got around and I often found myself working solo. I like to think it was more *passion* than *pushiness*, but I never let a night go by without telling someone about my newly discovered Jesus. One night "Ted" was trapped in a truck with me while I spewed Scripture. Mid-sermon on Sin, Salvation, and the Second Coming my victim shot his hand up like a cop stopping traffic and said, "Enough!" I got the message and from then on I reduced my sermons down to two, instead of three, points.

The gospel is *"the power of God for salvation,"*[45] and it's our privileged duty to share it[46]. Since he has done all the real work to win people's affection we don't have to be so uptight about getting them from point A to B to C.

It's not only unnecessary; it's counterproductive when we turn the fireman's hose of spiritual verbiage on people who just need to sip the Water of Life. Of course, we want to bring people all the way to a radical conversion on the spot, and there's nothing better when that happens. But when that doesn't occur, I consider it a minor victory to be at least one Christian that might not get listed under the heading of "Self-Righteous Know-It-Alls." If I can't win everybody to Jesus, I want to at least give him or her no new alibis for rejecting him.

Sometimes it's best to lower the bar of how we measure "successful conversations" about Jesus. When my son was doing some substitute teaching at a high school, his bottom-line mantra each day was: "No one gets hurt and nothing catches fire!" He assured me that most days he achieved both goals. If you're going to share Christ with people, at least try not to hurt anyone!

People need to know that we're friends whether or not they decide to follow Jesus. I've been talking to a friend about the Lord for a few years now. All along, while I've been trying to point "Robert" toward Jesus, he's made every effort to convince me that Jesus is passé and his idea of the divine is far superior to mine. He seems more intent on "evangelizing" me than I am him, and his "evangelistic" efforts toward me are usually done in a combative tone.

Recently he said, "I tell you and tell you but you don't listen!" He can be downright rude and I've told him so. He went on to say that he didn't want to hang out anymore if I wasn't going to embrace his "theology" and, as he says, "get past the Jesus thing." I told him that wasn't going to happen and that it was a bit discouraging for me too in my efforts to nudge him toward Jesus. Furthermore, I told him that I hoped we could still be friends, and that I genuinely cared about him as a person, not just as a potential convert.

He didn't immediately warm to the idea, but after he thought about it awhile he said that friendship was possible. Of course I want him to come to Jesus, but arguing with him sure wasn't working and I do really want us to be friends. It also seems the better part of wisdom to maintain some proximity with him while waiting patiently for him to respond to the Spirit's work in him.

We might do well to celebrate the smaller steps people need to take toward a friendship with God. Remember that we're *not their first clue* that he exists (creation, conscience, culture, etc. all beat you to the punch) and we probably won't be their last. Our passion, then, can be a more *patient passion* to bring them to Jesus.

It helps me remember that I work *with* him and not just *for* him.

I get to work alongside of him in his grand friend-making scheme. Knowing that I'm simply appealing to the Spirit's attractive pull already going on in a person's soul relieves me of an unbearable weight on my shoulders. I can be less scripted in my efforts and a little more agile in my interactions. My witnessing then becomes more of a *collusion* and less of a *collision!*

It helps me have a relaxed urgency about sharing Christ.

Since it's not *on* me or *about* me, I can be more chill about telling others what I know about him.

Some people are so perfectly comfortable with their faith that they feel no need to hide it or to prove it. It's just who they are, so when they offer Jesus to others, it doesn't come out all forced and sweaty. They're just letting someone in on the "secret" of what makes them tick.

We can't witness to anyone the Spirit hasn't already been witnessing to, so our witness is more of a *follow-up call* than a *cold call*. It's like telling people more than they already know about what they already know in their knower.

The Spirit has been delivering his lines and directing the play long before I ever came on stage, and he'll continue playing his part long after I exit. My lines are important to be sure, but if I don't deliver them perfectly or skip something in the script, it doesn't ruin the whole play. God loves people way too much to hinge their eternal destiny on the quality of my performance.

Do we want them to know him and enjoy him as much as we do (or more)? Absolutely. But so does the Spirit; and he's doing all he can to captivate their hearts, so let's join him in his *easy yoke* and *light burden*.

It helps me listen more and download less.

The Spirit doesn't need us, but he does choose to use us. If, before we get our hands on people, we recognize God's hand is already on them, we tend to be less patriarchal and preachy. Our evangelistic efforts then look more Socratic than posturing. C.S. Lewis described himself as *"a fellow patient in the same hospital who, having been admitted a little earlier, could give some advice."*

Many years ago "Frank" and I were sharing the Lord with students on a college campus. Not willing to waste time with trivialities I would bum-rush people with a mouthful of spiritual expertise. Several times in a row he interrupted me mid-preach and asked them something like, *"So, what're your thoughts about God?"* At first, I was irritated by the disruption, until I realized there was a method to his madness. Not only was he rescuing them from my sermonizing, he knew that God was already working in them and the only way to find out what he was doing was to ask. Wow, what a concept!

We Christians tend to be better at telling people what they should believe rather than taking time to listen to what they already believe. We're like the mechanic that rushes into working on the car before hearing what's wrong with it. As foreign missionaries in a post-Christian culture, rather than merely bombarding them with words, we're more effective if we begin by listening to those we're befriending.

It's better to ask questions than to give answers to questions they aren't asking. How else can we know what the Spirit is already doing in them? And how else can we speak *to* them more and *at* them less? A good rule of thumb is to lead with listening and proceed with Jesus.

When highlighting all the questions that Jesus asked people in just one of the Gospels I nearly ran out of highlighter before running out of Gospel. He was God, and though he had important things to say, he asked them a lot of questions. I suppose he did this to get them engaged in conversation, provoke them to ponder how they might apply his message to their own lives, and so he could address their own personal issues. Seems like a pretty good strategy.

In his passionate pursuit of people God is always first on the scene preparing their hearts to grab hold of his love. At birth, Rahabs of all shapes and sizes are fitted with a supernatural wonder, and throughout their lives the Spirit nurtures it. Under his supervision, Creation, Conscience, Culture, Crises, and Creeds combine to cultivate this intrigue about the divine. While all the citizens of Jericho had some measure of "eternity in their hearts," at least one person displayed a sort of "pre-faith" in the truth about Yahweh.

An obvious collector of friendship invitations, it seems that Rahab was in the process of considering her RSVP when the scouts rang her doorbell. The two men were quite likely startled by how much revelation this pagan prostitute already possessed before they said a word.

Granted, to call what the scouts did "evangelism" in the classic sense of the word is a bit of a stretch. That they influenced her toward Yahweh was, at least at the first, purely inadvertent. They were there to do something else entirely and wound up "witnessing" to her.

I'll unpack that thought in the next chapter, but suffice to say that creation, conscience, etc. can only do so much to install eternity into the hearts of God's beloved. The best they can do is project an opaque image of the God of the Bible on their soul screen. The ubiquitous clues that he leaves need clarifying. And that's where we come in.

PART TWO

Accidental Evangelism

I'm certainly not implying that Joshua's two scouts had any intention of making Canaanite converts in Jericho. They were on a mission, but not necessarily one to win souls. Though the Spirit prearranged it, for their part, their influence on Rahab appears to have been purely serendipitous.

My sense is that they were more surprised by Rahab's receptivity and "pre-faith" than she was by their visit. It's not like they went to Jericho to go "witnessing." They weren't out walking the streets on a Saturday afternoon outreach. Joshua's instructions were to "*Go, look over the land,*" not go door to door with tracts inviting people to church. Yet, by God's design, their reconnaissance operation morphed into a saving encounter with an openhearted prostitute.

That's the way it works sometimes. Our flight plan and the Spirit's are typically dissimilar. Problem is, changing course from *our plan* in order to get on course with *his plan* isn't always as easy as it sounds. Inconveniences aside, what could be more important than being in the right place at the right time for a divinely scheduled appointment, especially if it involves influencing someone toward the Maker?

We were created to "do good works which God prepared in advance for us to do."[47] "Eternally Ordained Opportunities" is what I call these works that God providentially prepared in eternity past. In other words, he puts Rahabs in our path and gives us the opportunity to partner with him in his quest to befriend them.

Joshua's scouts were out doing recon of the land when they ran into a Spirit-prepared pre-christian (so to speak). What might've seemed accidental to them was actually an eternally ordained opportunity. The Spirit had already scanned the landscape, found a hungry-hearted prostitute, and then supernaturally delivered his unsuspecting "evangelists" to her door.

Most of my divine appointments with *Rahabs* are purely accidental on my part. Of course there are times when I'm actually aware of some prompting of the Spirit, but mostly I just try to live responsibly before God and trust that he'll orchestrate the unforeseen.

We can't very well take credit for being spiritual or strategic when we're just out "looking over the land" and he puts us in touch with someone with a spacious spirit.

When standing on top of buried treasure the best thing to do is start digging!

You probably noticed that Rahab initiated the conversation regarding her rescue. The scouts didn't bring it up. They merely responded to her proposal of making a deal for her salvation. That's not how it always goes but some people are just so ready for salvation that our role is to simply walk down the path that the Spirit has already carved out.

Rahabs of all types reside, recreate, and work in all our spheres of influence. They may not, at first glance, look like the "sort of persons" that anyone would most likely to become Christians, but that's the essence of the adventure of joining God in his quest for friends. He uses all kinds of people to invite all kinds of people to become his friends.

How could we ever know about anyone's spiritual disposition if we aren't willing to look past their exterior and delve into what's beneath? Like the scouts, we're on a treasure hunt for uncut diamonds, looking beyond their off-putting exterior and tuning into the deep treasure within. As Solomon mused, *"The purposes of a person's heart are deep waters, but a person of understanding draws them out."*[48]

There is a *depth* to Rahabs of every color and creed with whom we come into contact, something more profound than we might perceive at first glance. They may not yet perceive it, but they've got something deep inside them—someone to be, some life to live, something to contribute to the culture. It's up to us to help them discover their submerged treasure and use it for the glory of God and the good of people.

Though we're all susceptible to living shallow lives, essentially we are beings capable of living lives of immeasurable worth. Most people have lost hope for meaning and need to be provoked to believe that they're not merely what they appear to be on the *outside*. They may live primarily from—and/or for—their exterior, unaware that they even possess an *inner part,* let alone how to tap into it. Yet each human contains as much sunken treasure as everyone else to be brought up from the depths. They may have never peered below their own surface, but it's there.

For most, the treasure is covered by years, even generations, of the silt and sand of neglect. The gold is obscured and appears as a nondescript bulge on the ocean floor. It's up to us, as "people of understanding," to work alongside the Spirit to provoke them to pursue the true worth of their deeper part and bring it to the surface.

Rahab encounters and conversions are nothing short of miraculous. That God put the scouts in the home of such a serious seeker (possibly the only one in the city) should inspire us to trust him for the same sort of recurring miracle in our interaction with **Rahabs** in our own spheres of influence. We should be constantly on the lookout for people to whom the Spirit has been singing his love song. We listen for the music, however faint it might be, and join in the serenade.

As an example of reaching a Rahab by accident, one Sunday I gave a message on sharing Christ in our church and at the conclusion I asked everyone to pair up with someone and do a role-play evangelistic conversation. Twenty minutes later James brought a beaming teenage girl over to me, "This is 'Mitsy,'" he said. "She just gave her life to Jesus!"

"Cool," I said, thinking he meant that she played the role of unbeliever and that his mock conversation was successful.

He sensed from my tone that I didn't get it, "No. I mean she actually just received Jesus!"

He explained that she was the babysitter that we had hired that morning and since there were no kids in the nursery, she sat in the back and listened to the service. When everyone else was taken, James went over to her and asked her to join in the exercise. She complied and when he asked her if she wanted to give her life to Jesus, she said "Yes! For reals, yes!"

Another Rahab reached by accident! You have to love God's sense of timing, if not of good humor.

The Wordless Witness

You've probably heard the famous saying by Francis of Assisi, "Preach the gospel at all times and when necessary use words." I thought preaching was, by definition, a verbal thing! How does one *say* something without words?

Joshua found a way when he obeyed God and banned all speech while they marched around the city wall. Without words the Hebrew army "said" something to the fearful residents of Jericho. Apart from standard protocol they communicated.

"Okay everyone! Before we start this weeklong march around Jericho," shouted Joshua to his troops, *"here are a few ground rules. Don't say a word the whole week. Not a word!"* (Joshua 6:10)

Right. Wait! What?

Strange battle plan—even stranger as a method of evangelism!

What's the takeaway? Here are a few suggestions about *wordless witnessing.*

Wordless witnessing by listening

Notice that the two men didn't barge in to Rahab's home with threats of Yahweh's impending judgment. Instead, when they paused to listen to her, they understood that she was well aware of what was coming. The storm that was brewing outside their walls was no surprise to her. They knew this because they listened.

Hence, in her case, how unnecessary it would have been for them to present her with some pre-fab speech on God and judgment. She didn't need to be held over hell's flames in order to convert, which is not to say that some people don't need this. "Be merciful to those who doubt;" says Jude, "snatch others from the fire and save them; to others show mercy, mixed with fear."[49] When we truly listen, we learn that there's no one-size-fits-all approach to sharing Jesus with people.

There's only one gospel, but there's more than one way to share it. You wouldn't want your doctor to rush to a diagnosis and treatment of your condition before listening to your description of your pain. That's a formula for the unnecessary removal of some necessary parts!

When we do all the talking and expect others to do all the listening we tend to provide answers to questions they're not asking. That's not what I call being a good witness.

A person can say a lot by listening, especially if they listen with the intent to understand rather than with the intent merely to reply. One of the best gifts we can give to people is the gift of attention. Maybe we should advertise in our churches or set up tables on street corners that say: "Free Attention Giveaways!"

Of course, it's just as important to pay attention to the Spirit at the same time. That way we'll be aware of his prompts to "insert this thing or that..." Jesus said, *"Consider carefully how you listen."*[50] If we'll listen carefully to him and to Rahab simultaneously—one ear to heaven and the other to earth—we will be most apt to deliver good news in the best way possible.

Some of my friendship quest encounters are with the most mentally tangled up Rahabs who have long and involved conversations with themselves and invisible antagonists on street corners and public parks. You couldn't tell it by outward appearance, but, like Jericho's *least favorite daughter,* these profoundly troubled folks contain the image of their Creator and are beloved in heaven, where, if they arrive there someday, their minds will be reassembled and functional. In the meantime, these precious souls need to be shown authentic and affectionate attention, which is sometimes best done by restraining ourselves and simply listening to their ranting.

God tends to use our ears before he employs our mouths in our service to others. Especially with the most broken and confused, if we begin with honest and caring attention, the Spirit might find a way to use us to make an invisible, inaudible connection between his heart and theirs.

You can probably recall a time or two when Jesus patiently listened to your panic and paranoia. Think of this then as your very own "ministry of listening" as modeled after his.

We're to *"offer the parts of our body to God as instruments of righteousness."*[51] I assume that would include our ears as much as any other body part. As we serve people through listening we offer our ears to God for him to use in any way he can to influence people toward him.

On to the next way to witness wordlessly…

Wordless witnessing by Christ-like actions

> *"We should preach as though we're serving and serve as though we're preaching."*
> — **Jim Henderson**

It would be a little too stretchy for me to make an attempt to tether this point to the Rahab story, but it's a point I can't afford to ignore, so I'll be brief.

Jesus said, *"They will see your good works"*—not necessarily hear your good words—*"and glorify your Father in heaven."*[52] Peter echoed the same in his letter to spiritual exiles: *"Live such good lives among the pagans that… they may see your good deeds and glorify God on the day he visits us."*[53]

Yes, actions done in humility and love do count as evangelism. Doing good works just *for the heaven of it,* that is, not for the sake of impressing anyone, but simply for the love of God, is one brand of inadvertent kingdom influence. When people see us actually acting like Jesus—hopelessly loving God and tangibly demonstrating love toward people—whether we realize it or not, we're witnessing without words.

We didn't know we were witnessing to an on-looking neighbor when we picked up another neighbor's garbage that was strewn in their yard by the storm the night before. We weren't aware anyone was watching our reaction to the tongue-lashing the boss unleashed on us by the water cooler, but they were and they took note. We weren't showing off or trying to win converts when we stop most days on our way into the office and give that homeless guy who stations himself there a sandwich. We were just trying to act like Jesus, and beyond our notice, people observed our "good works" and were incrementally serendipitously attracted to our God.

Living in a righteous way is witnessing, albeit unconscious witnessing. We're not thinking, "I'm witnessing right now." We love Jesus so we consciously try to live in a way that pleases him, but we're not always conscious that living this way is a witness to onlooking pre-christians.

"I wanted to write and tell you that you really had an impact on my life," began a letter I received from a guy that I had hardly known a decade before. "I'm in prison for life," he wrote, "and I've become a Christian partially due to your witness." He went on, "You probably didn't know it but when you broke up that fight on the street and saved that guy from a beat down, a seed was planted." He was right. I didn't know what impact I had.

I did, however, recall the incident he was referring to. I was driving by when I saw "Carlos" and his friend pummeling a stranger in front of a liquor store. Before I stopped to think it over, I pulled my Volkswagen up on the sidewalk, jumped out and started screaming at them to stop. Let me be clear, all the other players were younger, bigger, and much tougher than me—so this was more an act of stupidity than of bravery.

While reading the letter, I racked my soggy brain for any memory of actually "witnessing" to Carlos. I couldn't remember sharing with him about Jesus, but something from the encounter that day must have stuck in his craw, sufficient to write me about his conversion.

"Peacemaking" is one of those things by which we are recognized as God's children.[54] I guess that's what happened that day––a purely inadvertent testimony. You might say, since there was some yelling on my part, it wasn't an entirely "wordless" witness!

Of course, there are countless other forms of the "good works" witness. Suffice it to say that when you do anything for others for the glory of Jesus in the name of Jesus you're being a witness for Jesus.

When we love one another and invite Rahabs into our circle we exercise yet another form of the wordless witness.

Wordless witnessing through a loving community

Fast-forward to after their rescue, Rahab and her family were welcomed into the Israelite community.

> "Joshua spared Rahab the prostitute, with her family and all who belonged to her ... and she lives among the Israelites to this day."
> — (Joshua 6:25)

Joshua didn't just set them adrift to fend for themselves but gave them a new and far better home among God's people. Theirs was no reluctant arm's-length arrangement with the Jews. They received this pagan prostitute into their community. She went on to marry one of their citizens and have children, the descendants of which were ancestors of Jesus.[55] There could be no clearer example of an outsider becoming an insider!

Elaine Heath said, "The proper context for evangelism is authentic Christian community, here the expression of loving community is the great apologetic for the gospel." Especially in our day of frayed social fabric, authentic community is itself evangelistic. It's an indispensible component of our wordless witness.

Inviting people to a church service is a *good* thing; welcoming them into friendship and community is even *better*. Our genuine relationships show the good news way more effectively than our services ever could, even with their impressive music and inspiring oratory.

Genuine community preaches. The ancient church practiced such community that thousands were drawn into its gravitational pull (Acts 2:42-47). This was no church growth strategy but an attractive lifestyle.

Marginalized Rahabs of all sizes, sexual preferences and social standings, lonely urbanites, and Millennials adrift intrinsically hunger for more than a bulletin and a balcony seat from which to watch the Sunday morning production. Whether or not they realize it, they have an internal need to belong.

Speaking of "belonging," the sequence to which I once subscribed was: People first *believe*, then *belong*, then *become*; i.e. get saved, then join the church, then begin growing in your faith. While it might well happen that way for many, I'm finding that a lot of folks, Rahab-like people in particular, need to *belong*—maybe for quite a while—before they come to savingly *believe* in Jesus and begin *becoming* more like him.

We have to keep an open mind about such things, pretty much everything when the Spirit is involved—that Spirit who comes and goes like wind.[56]

Our goal is for people to trust Jesus for salvation, yet many people have to first learn to trust and be trusted, love and be loved. Through many shipwrecked relationships and a cutthroat culture their "truster" has been damaged and can best be repaired in loving community.

The deck was stacked against Rahab being included into the Jewish community, which makes her inclusion all the more shocking. They had laws against such things and wouldn't be easily persuaded to overlook them. But they did. And when they did, the community immediately improved. She both benefitted *from* the community and became a benefit *to* the community. After all, she helped bring Jesus to the table![57]

Not judging someone who is different from us is not enough. We have to learn to include them into our lives and love them for Jesus—even before they trust in him. Our motto should be, "We welcome you to the table. Whether or not you decide to believe, you belong."

[I'm not proposing that we offer church membership or leadership positions for any and all comers. The *belonging* I'm speaking of has nothing to do with church politics or governance, but has everything to do with relationship. After all, we are on a friendship quest, not a membership drive.]

I've seen this happen in real time when people, like my friend Clyde, are attracted to the Christian community before being drawn to Christ.

The pastor had given a message and asked people who wanted to receive Jesus to come forward—something we used to do in church services. I approached Clyde at the altar, got briefly acquainted with him, and asked why he came forward. "What brought you to this point?" With all my theological training I expected him to confess that he was a sinner and wanted forgiveness and a changed heart. It was clear that he wanted these as well, but he indicated that what compelled him to respond was the loving family he observed in our church community. He wanted in on it!

He did receive forgiveness and a transformed life, but what caught his attention was the community that he longed for. Our church was witnessing to him without knowing it. We were just going about loving each other, he noticed, and he came to find out how he could be included. Clyde, a passionate follower of Jesus for over forty years now, was won by the power of the wordless witness called love.

"By this everyone will know that you are my disciples, if you love one another."[58]

The Disarming Power of Reluctant Humility

> *"Kindness has converted more sinners than zeal, eloquence, or learning."*
> — **Frederick William Faber**

Humility goes a long way as a form of *accidental evangelism*. The genuinely humble Christian is more apt to attract people toward the meek and humble Son of God, than the bluster of a self-styled God expert.

In their interaction with Rahab, the scouts display nary a note of privilege or conceit. They could very well have taken a superior and threatening tone with Rahab but they approached her on equal ground.

It helped that their relationship with her was mutually advantageous. They needed her as much as she needed them, which is something we ought always to keep in mind in all our relationships, including those with pre-Christians. Otherwise we come across as paternalistic and preachy.

There are two motives to try to get people to change their minds about God, pride and love. We either need to prove we're right (and them wrong) or we genuinely care about them and want them to have what we have.

Too many of our conversations look more like posturing and a battle of egos than good news telling. Neither defensive nor offensive Christians win many over to Jesus' side.

"He may use you to draw others to Himself" wrote Jeanne Guyon to French mystic Fenelon. "The people God uses are those who do not stand in His way because they have been made pure and transparent."

Granted, the first rule of humility is that you can never claim it for yourself. Once you do you're disqualified. Therefore, I claim to possess no large number of shares of the characteristic. If I contain any humble pieces at all they're unfinished and fleeting. With that admission in mind, allow me to tell a story of one of those fleeting moments. [A more complete account can be found in my Memoir called, *The Other End of the Dark*.][59]

When I broached the subject of Jesus with a Rahab-like homeless friend of mine he bristled at the thought of a God who would do nothing to protect his own Son from a brutal crucifixion. He was visibly upset over it.

When I started to explain why Jesus did what he did, my explanation was uncharacteristically muddled. I thought it was weird since I can usually boil the gospel down to pretty graspable terms. But this time I couldn't quite get it out.

In my frustration, without any forethought, as though it wasn't even me speaking, I eked out an apology – "I'm really sorry, man. I'm not explaining this very well." I chalked it up to a loss and braced myself for him to take advantage of his "win" with some snarky remark.

I was stunned when he softened his tone and replied almost sympathetically, "That's OK, man. It must be hard to explain." Dazed, I went on to tell him about how much I love Jesus even if I couldn't explain him very well. We talked a few more minutes and parted ways.

It wasn't until later that I realized that he had more than a philosophical objection to Christianity that could be solved with clever apologetics. In this case, my sincere apology for an inadequate answer was more effective that day. When I lowered my defenses his surliness shrank and he lowered his Jericho wall just a little.

Satan, the most conceited being in the world, feeds on pride. "Pride," wrote C.S. Lewis, "is the complete anti-God state of mind." The best way to defeat arrogance is with meekness. My inadvertent response disarmed the spirit of pride and momentarily neutralized the adversary's efforts to keep him incarcerated behind his wall. The Spirit slightly lifted the spiritual barrier like venetian blinds and let a little sunshine in.

My evangelism was "accidental" in that it wasn't the words I said or the strategy I used. My acumen as a debater moved the conversation anywhere but forward. As surprising as it was to us both, only when I admitted failure to communicate, a shift occurred. Though he didn't decide to follow Jesus on the spot, it seemed to me that the Spirit coaxed him a little further in the general direction of the Father's love.

I don't recommend this as an evangelistic device, a sure-fire formula for soul winning. I just wonder how much better our testimony would be if we toned down the condescending rhetoric and approached people with genuine humility.

Let me be clear, humble doesn't mean timid. It means our confidence lies in the Spirit rather than from our knowledge, experience, or debating skills. "Courage," says Collin Hansen, "is not measured by how many people you can offend."

Peter, the apostle best known for his overconfident bluster, learned over time to share his hope in Christ with "gentleness and respect."[60] When we lack these qualities we tend to condescendingly answer questions they're not asking. Too many Christians are "seldom right but never in doubt!" Their mudslinging stump speech testimonies don't win many people but they do give them a commanding appearance.

Mother Teresa used to say, "Humility is nothing but the truth." It's not something we should have to convince ourselves of. It's an accurate assessment of how things are. It's the truth about how flawed we are and how fortunate we are for God to love us in spite of our flaws. Approaching people in that spirit goes a long way to influencing them toward the God of mercy.

One telltale sign of pride in our testimony is when we feel the need to go on and on, as though it's the profundity and sheer number of our words that convinces them to repent. By contrast, I've found that usually less is more...

Sometimes Less is More

*"When words are many, sin is not absent,
but he who holds his tongue is wise."*
— **Proverbs 10:19**

"Be quick to listen, slow to speak..."
— **James 1:19**

Remember how God told the Jews to march around the city walls for seven days without saying a word?[61] No speaking for a week! Now that would be a gargantuan miracle for mouthy me! I mean, not a word whispered between marchers, not even one tiny holler up to the Jerichoans peering down from their ramparts? "Do what I tell you," says the supremely capable Creator. "Rest your mouths for the moment. I don't need your help. I've got this!"

When I first started following Jesus it was more like him following me around cleaning up my messes. This includes my typical "witnessing" attempts, which entailed breathless barrages of words and Bible quotes. I reasoned that if I paused to inhale, my near comatose victims tended to rush home to open their junk mail.

I don't see Joshua's scouts giving long speeches to Rahab about Yahweh. Their conversation seems pretty straightforward. She tells them what she already knows and they listen. In fact, if you compare the volume of her words with theirs you'll find she says nearly twice as much as they do—not the customary proportions of most witnessing conversations, I'd say.

God doesn't merely recruit silver-tongued orators or skilled apologists for his quest for friends. Silver and skill sometimes actually inhibit the Spirit's efforts to find his way into a person's consciousness. They can detract from the actual good news itself.

Don Everts writes, "If they have just a thimbleful of curiosity, we could actually douse that small curiosity by answering their small, limited question with a hundred and one apologetic answers we've been waiting to 'use' on someone. Try not to dump five gallons of answers on a six-ounce question."[62]

If you've ever actually talked to a telemarketer for more than ten seconds you know that they operate under the assumption that if they just keep talking you'll cave in and buy whatever they're hawking. Those who subscribe to the *Sales Method of Evangelism* are not terribly dissimilar. They figure if they keep up the verbiage, their customers will eventually wear down and sign up to be saved! And don't think for a minute that people are any less put off by such manipulative methods than you are. Restraint is said to be the highest form of discipline.

One mechanic said to his customer, "I couldn't repair your brakes, so I made your horn louder." Christians with bad brakes (i.e. no pause button) and a loud horn (an off-putting bluster) attract few hungry souls to Jesus. Turning a fireman's hose on a shot glass is not the best way to fill it.

Sometimes your best bet is to keep your spiel simple—the more terse the more memorable. As opposed to ganging up on a person with a horde of nouns, verbs, and spiritual adjectives, sometimes fewer words can give greater weight to your testimony.

Saying less may leave room for the Spirit to interject his choice ideas into their minds and allow time for them to muse about them. There have been times when I've nearly felt a hand on my mouth, preventing me from saying as much as I wanted to say. It's like the Spirit says, *"You've said enough, Barney. Now let him think about it. Don't interrupt me."*

What about "apologetics"?

I don't know about you, but Jesus came into my *heart* before he entered my *head*. No one used on me the cosmological, ontological, or really much of any other logical arguments for God, which probably wouldn't have worked since I wouldn't have known what those words meant anyway. I had heard nothing about my depravity, his divinity, or the Bible's canonicity till well after I received Jesus. I just heard him knocking and I opened the door and learned some of that other stuff later.

This is not to say that there is no value in employing apologetics in our witness, especially with people whose Jericho wall is made of intellectual objections to the gospel. Every Christian should be able to intelligently and intelligibly "give reasons for the hope we have."[63]

That said, I usually lean away from an information-heavy witness. Not that many people are moved to faith by a four-step bullet-point proof for Intelligent Design or rhyming sermon points that promise a "blessed life." Our culture is glutted with slick pitches everywhere else and my guess is that most people are more interested in connecting with the eternal and living meaningful lives.

Of all people, the apologist and author of the classic work, *Evidence That Demands A Verdict,* Josh McDowell said, "The evidences did not bring me to Christ. The evidences got my attention, but it was God's love that drew me. It was the love I saw between a group of genuine believers who loved not only Jesus Christ but also each other—and even me! The evidence got my attention, but love drew me." [64]

Propositional answers to sincere questions can be very helpful at times, but it seems to me that most people (especially postmodern generations) want answers that are personal and grounded in real-life experience. They're not usually looking for, or particularly receptive to, philosophically satisfying answers. They want to know if we're for real and if our faith makes an actual difference in real life situations.

There's no doubt that apologetics helps some people overcome intellectual barriers to faith, but it's my experience that the most formidable wall is in the *will* rather than in the *head*. My suggestion then is to speak to their spoken and unspoken questions. When we respond with our life of faith instead of memorized clichés, and open ourselves and our honest struggles to our friends, we're showing them the gospel at work.

On behalf of their postmodern generation, university campus ministers, Don Everts and Doug Schaupp write: "We are more experiential than propositional in our connection to truth. We are more communal than individualistic. We value authenticity over theory. We understand struggle more than naive certainty."[65]

The artful witness wants to speak to the heart and the head. Realizing that some things can't be cognitively detected but must be spiritually discerned s/he, in order to increase their chances of getting to the heart of matter, will look to the Spirit to help them see beneath the surface. When we speak from the heart to the heart it's called "discernment." We cultivate discernment when we're willing to download less and listen more (to others and to the Spirit).

Believe me, I could have said more about this, but --- *sometimes less is more.*

PART THREE

It Takes a Savior To Save

I mentioned in the introduction how "Joshua" and "Jesus" both mean *Savior*. To my mind this implies at the very least an oblique correspondence between Jesus' commissioning his disciples to go out in pairs and bring people to him and Joshua directing his pair of scouts to rescue Rahab and bring her back to him. The disciples didn't save any people, but merely brought them to Jesus who did the saving. Similarly, the scouts were *witnesses*, not saviors. Their job was to bring Rahab and her family to Joshua as ours is to bring people to Jesus.

John says that, "the first thing Andrew did was to find his brother Simon and tell him, 'We have found the Messiah' (that is, the Christ). And he brought him to Jesus."[66] That's what we witnesses do. We bring people to the Savior and then let him do all the saving. We do the human thing and he does the divine.

Salvation is work cut out only for the divine. It's a miracle. Just as the supernatural surrounds every salvation, miracles brimmed over in Rahab's rescue. For instance, walls crumbling at the behest of shouts and trumpets? Not bad in the miracle department I'd say. Was it their perfectly articulated shouts or the trumpeters' unique tone that did the trick? I think not. No more than our perfectly articulated testimonies and sanctimonious tone that saves a soul.

To point out the miraculous nature of someone's conversion, Jesus told a parable:

> *"This is what the kingdom of God is like. A man scatters seed on the ground. Night and day, whether he sleeps or gets up, the seed sprouts and grows, though he does not know how."*
> — (Mark 4: 26-27)

One thing for sure is that we aren't in the business of creating life or changing hearts. We can't know which seed will take root and which will bounce off a stony heart. We can't control the process or manipulate someone into salvation. We might be able to get them to say a prayer and convince them to cut down on their sinning, but to get them to come savingly to Jesus is out of our league.

Jim Henderson speaks of "non-manipulative intentionality"[67] which I take to mean that though we do and say all we can to connect someone to Jesus, we are obliged to be uncontrived and refuse to use manipulation to get them there. Control-freak Christians need not apply.

We have to admit that the seed is still a mystery to us, and though we don't really know how it works, we toss it out there in hopes that it'll take. It's not our job to predict or control the mystery of the seed, but to sow it and so trust the Spirit to make it grow even in our sleep!

The parable has a great ending:

> "All by itself the soil produces grain— first the stalk, then the head, then the full kernel in the head. As soon as the grain is ripe, he puts the sickle to it, because the harvest has come."
> — (MARK 4:28-29)

The smart farmer observes the different organic stages of growth that are out of his/her control and acts accordingly. S/he sows the seed, patiently waters and cares for it while it germinates and develops into a plant, and then harvests it when it's ready.

Salvation is a miraculous thing and can't be rushed. When we hurry someone along into a premature confession of faith we do more damage than good. The best thing we can do is discern their spiritual readiness and, with the help of the Spirit, introduce them to Jesus!

Jesus didn't come here to start a new religion called "Christianity," so our testimony is about him and not our religion. Christianity is a construct; the way we organize, categorize, and theologize. But at the end of the day it's Jesus who saves, and our witness of *him* so much more compelling than any construct.

We're immersed in a friendship that we want everyone to experience. "We proclaim to you," wrote the disciple whom Jesus loved, "the eternal life… that has appeared to us… what we have seen and heard, so that you also may have fellowship with us. And our fellowship is with the Father and with his Son, Jesus Christ."[68]

In many ways we have handcuffed Jesus to traditions, doctrines, and dogma. Certainly, there is a place for those, but they're not Jesus and can't save anyone. Our goal is not to download into people all the right ideas and make "Christians" out of them. We want them to follow Jesus and fall as hopelessly in love with him as we are (or more hopelessly).

He is our message. We invite people to be "reconciled" to *him*,[69] not to a religion or a church. We don't have to clarify Christianity, answer for the Crusades, solve the problem of Original Sin, and defend the history of the church. There will be a time for them to sort out exactly what they believe, their doctrines and dogmas. But our goal is to introduce them to Jesus.

Convinced that Jesus was the Savior, the woman at the well invited her community to *"Come see a man,"*[70] not "Come hear a sermon." She had just then been "gospeled" by Jesus and before she had the time to become theologically proficient she was gospeling others with the only thing she knew, *"Come to Jesus."*

Christianity as a construct is to many people like a house with a sign on it that says, "Christianity: Do Not Enter!" On the contrary, the house into which we invite people is the house of Jesus. He's at the door (more accurately, he *is* the Door)[71] inviting people into his house. "He's not the guy in the way. He *is* the way."

Meanwhile, back in Jericho, another wonder worth noting presented itself the day of Rahab's rescue. We're told that her house was built into the city wall,[72] which likely would have eased her regular clients' undetected exit from her establishment. So when the wall fell, how did her house not fall with it? She and her family obeyed what they were told and held up in the house when everything around them crumbled. Though I've heard a number of theories, I really couldn't say for sure how it worked. Did every other section of the wall fall, leaving her house standing on stilts? All I know is, like salvation, it bore the obvious mark of the miraculous.

I'm saying that the saving thing that God does is light years above our pay grade. His rescue mission is a supernatural act. Depending on our ability to "save" people is a fool's errand. We have zero talent for it. We *live in God's story* and we *tell his story*, but he's the one who pulls people into the narrative. He's been at work in people way before we met them, sets up the timing for us to share our lives with them, and when it's time to actually do the "born-again-ing," he does all that too!

As we've seen, Rahab was so primed to seek the Lord before the two men showed up that she approached them with her proposal of rescue. Since the stories about God had reached her town well before the people of God arrived, they didn't have to pull out the hard sell. She was convinced before they even arrived at her door that trouble was coming. I'd say theirs was a pretty painless "evangelistic" encounter.

Let's be honest, it's not always this easy. Most people, repeated enticements of the Spirit notwithstanding, are less than enthused about handing over the reins of their lives to Someone they can't even see. Therefore, if we hope to reach reachable *Rahabs* we have to be willing to be rejected most times. Since we can't predict people's readiness to receive the truth, we have to risk it and give the Spirit something to work with.

No, it doesn't always happen quite so easily as in Rahab's case. But we should give the gospel itself[73] and our personal story a little more credit, and the Spirit's serenade a little more opportunity to find its way into their consciousness.

Savior Sellers?

> "I have seen the gospel treated like a product on a late-night infomercial... As soon as they sense you're not interested in buying, they dismiss you and it's on to the next potential buyer."
> — Dan Kimball[74]

> "You received without paying, now give without being paid."
> — Matthew 10:8 (Good News Translation)

As I've indicated before, Joshua's two agents weren't there in Rahab's house to "buy" anything. To this I would add, neither did they come to "sell" something. When the topic of her rescue came up, they merely offered her an escape from what was coming. They weren't Savior-sellers.

To be honest, salespeople scare me. I usually avert my eyes when someone with a hard sell lurks near. I figure if our eyes don't meet they can't guilt me into buying something I don't need. Car salespeople are the scariest. The "I'm-just-browsing" response doesn't seem to dissuade those in the hunt for "Salesman of the Month" award.

I've noticed people using the same eye-contact-avoidance tactic when the God topic comes up in conversation. They can tell when we're just trying to make a sale. Having been marketed into a sales stupor they can't stand even one more pitch. Their eyes glaze over, their ears close, and their brains tune out whenever they detect our self-serving motives and want no part of what we're "selling."

I've heard some presentations of the good news that sounded terribly similar to billboard guarantees: "If you come to Jesus he will get you that job, win you that wife, or heal you of cancer!" Maybe he will and maybe he won't, but unless the Spirit clearly compels you, don't make promises on his behalf. His is a "gospel to the poor" but it doesn't come, as gospel grifters would indicate, with a guaranteed path to riches.

"Evangelism as a method, is dangerous," says Carl Medearis, "because it's something we 'do' to other people. Nobody likes to be 'done.'"[75] A woman was struggling to get her dog to take some medicine. She lifted him up in her arms in a vain attempt to shove it down his throat. He squirmed and fussed until she dropped him and the medicine on the kitchen floor. At which point he lapped it all up. He didn't mind the medicine; he just didn't like the way she was giving it to him! Delivery is important.

A change of paradigm might serve to improve the effectiveness of our witness. Instead of Gospel salespersons we might better think of ourselves as spiritual **"Tour Guides."** It's not like we're selling anything and trying to profit from it, anyway. Right? Our job is to share what we've found and tell people where they can find it—for free!

My favorite tour guides are the ones who introduce me to fascinating places and invite me into their fascination. They've seen the site and given their spiel hundreds of times, yet the allure of it hasn't waned and their joy in sharing it remains infectious. Worth every penny of the cost of the tour is the guide that is still enamored with his or her subject matter.

Or we might think of ourselves as **"Matchmakers"** for Jesus. He's the perfect match for—well—everyone! Our job is to try to get them together and leave the rest to love. Paul came close to calling us matchmakers:

> *"We're Christ's representatives. God uses us to persuade men and women to drop their differences and enter into God's work of making things right between them. We're speaking for Christ himself now: Become friends with God; he's already a friend with you."*
> — **2 Corinthians 5:20 (The Message)**

If you can tolerate a final alternative to Savior-selling, we might think of sharing Christ as a matter of **"Show & Tell."** You remember that assignment in elementary school to show your classmates something special to you and tell them about it. You carted your puppy to class in a cardboard box. You took her out of the box and held her in your arms in front of the class and told them all about her and how much you loved her.

Showing and sharing, that's how we introduce our friends to our Friend Jesus. We *show* him off by the way we live and *tell* people why we live that way as best we can.

Though they're inextricably linked, some of us do a lot more *sharing* than *showing*. We try to get away with *telling* about Jesus without taking the trouble to bring him to class. Our assignment though is not "Show OR Tell." No wonder people get bored with just our telling. We've brought no visual aid, no puppy!

Rule of thumb: If it doesn't *show*, don't *tell!*

We witness with two hands: Practice and Proclamation. Amputate one of those hands and the message becomes garbled, even oxymoronic.

I would remind us that we can't get away with just *showing it*, we also have to *tell it*. It's not good enough to just stand in front of the class holding the puppy. We need to tell something about her.

Most people who don't follow Jesus haven't yet been fully introduced to him. That's our job, to make an adequate introduction through words and works.

By the way, Jesus did NOT say, "They will see your *good looks* and glorify your Father in heaven." It's not our *good looks* that verify that ours is a salvation made in heaven. Our witness has nothing to do with good-looking Christians or good-looking churches with impressive presentations. Our "good works" have to do with the way we conduct ourselves in the world as lovers of Jesus.

Being witnesses is not an either/or proposition. We've failed if they can't hear our words past the noise of our lives. We have to both *live* and *give* a good testimony.

Winning, Not Wounding

> "As we argue, we can deceive ourselves
> into thinking we are actually serving them,
> helping them along toward Jesus, but
> often this reactionary posture actually
> works to derail their journey of faith."
> — **Don Everts**[76]

> "Let your conversation be gracious
> and attractive so that you will have
> the right response for everyone."
> — **Colossians 4:6**

You'll notice that Joshua's scouts didn't tie up Rahab and whisk her away to their camp against her will. They didn't threaten, cajole, or strong-arm her into leaving Jericho and coming back with them. They simply offered to rescue her from her doomed existence and to include her in their community. This is how we win people to Jesus. We *captivate* them not take them captive.

Allow me a brief detour from the Rahab storyline in order to look at an incident in the New Testament that illustrates, by negative example, a *wounding*, as opposed to a *winning* approach to faith-sharing. We'll get back to the main road momentarily, but, in light of our desire to be the best witnesses we can be, I just can't resist retelling an episode in the life of one of my favorite Bible characters.

Peter was present in the garden on the night Jesus was arrested. He and his friends slept through the prayer meeting and woke up whacking off a guy's ear! Among other things, this wacky story teaches us how *not* to make friends with God.

How *Not* to Win People

> *"There is no issue that is worth debating with a non-Christian if it could possibly hinder them from entering into this relationship. What difference does it make what a person believes about this or that story of the Bible, or how they vote, or whether they're gay, straight, or transgender, or whether they're a patriot of our country or of a country that is an enemy of ours, if they're not yet in a relationship with Christ?"*
> — **Gregory A. Boyd**[77]

> *"Lord, should we strike with our swords?" And one of them struck the servant of the high priest, cutting off his right ear. But Jesus answered, "No more of this!" And he touched the man's ear and healed him.*
> — **Luke 22:49-51**

This is a case of a "sinner in the hands of an angry Christian"! Not good.

A lot of people think Jesus is pretty cool, but his Church—not so much. Go figure! Could their aversion have anything to do with how we approach them by *cutting off* communication with them? (Pun intended.) After what Peter did, Malchus couldn't very well "hear" the good news, at least not from *him*. Let's just say that an outreach strategy that leaves people bleeding out of the side of their head is not a particularly good one.

Though not the last, or even the worst, of Peter's impetuosity, it was his most theatrical. Assault with a deadly weapon is not included the apostle's job description! For the time being he would be God's poster boy for how *not* to influence people toward Jesus.

Of course the central story is Jesus' ear-replacing wonder, his last miracle before the cross. It seems to me like a waste to spend it on fixing something one of his generals broke; but then again, that's Jesus.

Peter doesn't get a pass for assaulting an unarmed man just because it ended well. An awful movie with a happy ending is still an awful movie. The *end* definitely didn't justify Peter's *means*. But this is one of those times we can all be glad that God works "all things" together for good.

Peter's recklessness illustrates how we act more like "witnesses for the prosecution" than for the defense. My recurring prayer is, *"Lord, I know I'm going to make mistakes but may they be small and seldom. If I hurt anyone, please heal them and, for your glory, win anyone I might have wounded."*

Our motives for sharing faith should never be to appease God, impress Christians, or oppress non-christians. "Don't be," says Brian McLaren, "the ecclesiastical counterpart of a mealtime telemarketer or email spammer barraging people with unwanted messages."

We're supposed to be *signposts* that point people toward Jesus not *stumbling blocks* that trip them up on their way. Even though Jesus' *miracle* compensated for Peter's *meltdown*, we shouldn't presume that God will use this same MO in every case. He's pretty busy as it is without having to mop up our messes.

"When we make sharing our faith a war of ideals," writes Carl Medearis, "we create casualties on both sides of the boundary."[78] If we're *wounding* more people than we're *winning* we should find a better way.

Attacking Hostages or the Hostage Taker?

> *"Put your sword back in its place,"*
> *Jesus said to him, "for all who draw*
> *the sword will die by the sword."*
> — **MATTHEW 26:52**

The Lord took a colossal risk to include *us* in his friendship quest, yet he sticks to his plan. His mercy notwithstanding, we have no excuse for misusing the opportunities and abilities he gives us. Just because we have a sword doesn't mean we're supposed to use it.

Sometimes we Christians forget who the enemy is and we attack the hostages rather than the *hostage takers* with the sword of our mouths. The Spirit's sword serves as *a surgical scalpel* to heal damaged souls as well as a *weapon of war* to defeat the enemy of our souls. It cuts through the most calloused conscience to make repairs in the diseased heart. But we must keep it scabbarded when we're tempted to hurt someone with it.

Derek Penwell said, *"Jesus didn't die so that we could win bar bets with other religions about who understands God best."* Just because we *can* win arguments with people about God doesn't mean we're *supposed* to. He didn't hire us to be his defense attorneys. You might be smarter, a better debater, and even more adequately informed than your "victims." But it doesn't please God or bring people closer to him when we assault them with "sharp" arguments.

It starts when they pull out the clobber questions. "How could Jesus be the only way? What's up with you Christians and gays? How do you explain the crusades?" We can't seem to let those go unanswered and we pull out our best rebuttals. Block the left jab and respond with a right cross. "Our Religion Can Beat Up Your Religion!" isn't the best header for your church sign.

Argumentative mode usually does more harm than good. We might just be derailing them rather than putting them on the right track that leads to Jesus. Plus, just when we think we've locked the argument down with our bullet-point logic, someone comes along with more logical points and better debating skills. That's a lose-lose.

"If evangelism by frontal-assault works," suggests Jim Henderson, "then let's all start carrying large signs that say, 'You are lost. You are bad! Ask me for help!'"[79] We're not "God's Gestapo" or witnesses for the prosecution, hired by God to bust everyone for their sin.

Witnessing angry is like giving someone a good kiss with bad breath! Ralph Moore said that our ability to reach people for Christ comes "in direct proportion to our ability to stop judging and to begin caring." Surely you've heard the adage: "People don't care how much we know until they know how much we care." I'm not talking about counterfeit caring for the purpose of winning a soul. I mean genuine compassion and love.

"Winning *over* someone" isn't the same as "winning someone over." It's Pharisaic pride that seeks to win debates *about* our "Joshua" (Jesus) rather than win people *to* him. Coming out on top in a theological debate usually just pushes people further away from God. The holiest thing we can do is surrender any compulsion for verbal jousting as an evangelistic tool. (It's purely coincidental if it sounds like I learned these things from any debacled evangelism attempts of my own!)

Ready, Fire, Aim! is not a good strategy for witnessing. The swing-first-and-ask-questions-later method is nothing if not painfully reminiscent of the ancient crusaders who slashed everything in their path and blamed it on Providence. We're supposed to serve people not stab them with the truth.

Since we Christians are more often identified by *what we hate* than by *how we love*, it's not entirely shocking that terms like: "Christian, Church, and Evangelical" in the pre-christian's lexicon are pejoratives. We've made it quite clear what we are *against* but we haven't shown them what we're *for*. Jesus wasn't identified as "that sin-hater." When he asked his disciples what people thought of him, Peter didn't say: "Some think you're against the Romans, others think you hate the Samaritans, others think you can't stand gays!"

Our rallying call is never to be "Man your battle stations!" Dan Kimball asks, "When you are studying apologetics, does your heart break in compassion for the people you are preparing to talk to? Or are you stockpiling ammunition to show them that they're wrong?"[80]

Though sometimes we have to debate the truth and even don the prophet's robe, but when we do, we must leave our sword at home. "No more of this!" Jesus scolded Peter. "Put the sword back in its place."

Calamitous evangelistic strategies notwithstanding, how might we proceed to persuade people in the general direction of our Friend?

How *Jesus* Wins People

I don't know about you, but Jesus won my heart, not by force but by fascination.

Note to self. Do what Jesus did!

He bent down, picked up Malchus' bloody ear, and tenderly reattached it. No fanfare or drumroll. He knew he would need that ear if he were going actually *hear* the Good News at some point.

Healing people is always a better gospeling technique than *hurting* them. Peter showed what he could do with a sword and Jesus showed what he could do with a touch. Definitely an improved method of outreach!

While Peter did his Lancelot imitation on a man he perceived as a threat, Jesus saw him as a man in need. Being more concerned about Malchus' welfare than his own, Jesus reached out and made him well—evangelism the Jesus way.

Jesus' "enemy love"[81] is always a better apologetic than the sword-swinging aggression of Peter. Compassionate service wields a power to affect people in ways that argumentative tactics never can. Jesus delayed his arrest to heal an enemy and later put a pause on dying in order to welcome a thief into his kingdom! That's how God makes friends.

This same spirit of selflessness marks authentic Good News-tellers. It's less about *defending* Jesus with a weaponized Bible than *demonstrating* him with the power of love.

But how do we download the kind of heart that fascinates people toward him?

Peter entered the garden that night in a spirit of self-reliance. Seeing this, Jesus afforded him and his two colleagues the opportunity to obtain the Father's heart and avoid the epic blunder he saw coming. He invited them to join him in his last prayer meeting.

Remember, brothers James and John (also in the garden that night) were no better at charming people toward Jesus than was Peter. They tipped their hand when they made a bid to edge the others out for the top posts in Jesus' administration (seats "at his right hand and left"). Not only that, these were the same two who volunteered to incinerate Samaritans with fire from heaven. While Peter's weapon of choice was a sword; theirs was lightening—neither are tools of the evangelism trade!

Eventually, schooled by the Spirit, all three exchanged their weapons for invitations. Peter came to understand that the lovingly wielded Spirit's sword is more effective than any soldier's blade. And the Sons of Thunder learned to love their enemies rather than cremate them!

Jesus invited these three to pray with him so they would experience what I call, *"a fellowship with the Father that fortifies us against falling."* "Watch and pray," he told his narcoleptic apprentices, *"so that you will not fall into temptation. The spirit is willing, but the flesh is weak."*[82]

Peter in particular seems to have had a proclivity for a recurring "impulse control disorder," the therapy for which Jesus prescribed was an hour of flesh-denying, spirit-strengthening prayer.

All three nodded off during prayer—three times! What happens when we drowse instead of casting our fears and cares on God? We retain our fears and rely on swordsmanship for protection and for the advancement of the cause of Christ. Prayerless Christians have been known to be some of the most reckless ones.

They napped through prayer and Peter woke up swinging. Had they spent time in the needed time in prayer that night instead of dozing, the story might have ended differently. Their *willing spirits* might have won over their *weak flesh* and garnered enough self-control to keep their swords scabbarded.

Even if we can't seem to pray for an hour it might be good if we just pause for a while, if for no other reason than to reduce our frenetic heart rate and thereby avoid less than productive evangelistic encounters.

Second Chances

Later that very night the Spirit gave Peter an opportunity to redeem himself when Malchus' nephew approached him in the high priest's courtyard and asked, "Didn't I see you with him in the garden?"[83]

Translation: *Aren't you that guy that attacked my Uncle and chopped his ear off? What the *%#@ is wrong with you? If that's how you people roll I want nothing to do with you! From now on stay away from me and my family!*

Not exactly the response we look for in our evangelistic efforts.

This was Peter's second chance to win Malchus—this time through his nephew. Wouldn't it have been cool had he said: *"Yeah, I was there. I totally screwed up and I regret it. I'm the one who should be going to prison instead of Jesus. Did you see what he did for your uncle? Give him another chance and you'll find out how amazing he is!"*

Instead, the rooster crowed. Second chance wasted! Peter's divine appointment passed him by. Been there, done that.

But thanks be to the God of many chances! Over time the Spirit transformed Peter from rash swordsman to wise ambassador. Trial and a ton of error taught him the kind of humility requisite for all friendship-making ambassadors for God.

By his picnic brunch with Jesus on the beach Peter was still as hangdog as a man can be. His heart had been aerated by failure and for the first time in his life he was fresh out of bluster when Jesus reaffirms his confidence in him—"feed my lambs."[84]

Some years later this same apostle with a humbled heart could say in good conscience: "Be ready to speak up and tell anyone who asks why you're living the way you are, and always with the utmost courtesy."[85]

It's that *utmost courtesy* part that Peter developed over time. It's difficult to be courteous and swing a sword at the same time!

Sometimes Do and Sometimes Don't

> *"As serious as the problem of overpushy witnesses may be, a related problem may be even more serious: the number of Christians who simply keep their faith to themselves and never share it with anyone."*
> — **Brian McLaren**

"Evangelizing" Rahab (so to speak) and including her into their Hebrew community is, what we might call, "out of the box" for the Jews of the day. This approach to their conquest and governance of the land didn't always include bringing non-Jews into their family of believers, especially not pagan prostitutes, and definitely not in this way. The whole "red rope" method, for instance, which we'll talk about later, was an entirely unprecedented method in rescue operations.

Advancing the influence of Yahweh's kingdom in such unusual ways is an example to us in our approach to offer Jesus to our friends.

King Solomon gave some seeming contradictory advice in successive sentences:

> *Do not answer a fool according to his folly,
> or you yourself will be just like him.*
> — **Proverbs 26:4**

Without taking a breath his very next counsel was to do the opposite . . .

> *Answer a fool according to his folly, or
> he will be wise in his own eyes.*
> — **Proverbs 26:5**

Wisdom, which was Solomon's main theme in Proverbs, is not necessarily discovering a silver bullet that always works in every case. Wisdom is not a static thing; instead it is dependent on a variety of considerations including the present leading of the Spirit. Without this wisdom we'll depend too heavily on routine and sterile gospel-sharing methods. This is why Solomon could claim, as we've previously pointed out, that it's the wise that "win souls."[86]

Jesus was notorious for varying his responses to people according the Spirit's leading, the unique circumstances, and the receptivity of his hearers. For instance, sometimes he proclaimed divine authority and sometimes he left it to his audience to come to their own conclusions about him. Sometimes he defended himself against persecutors and at other times he was mute.

His approach suited the circumstance and the person. He was harsh in the temple but gentle with the woman caught in adultery. He was slightly less flexible with his disciples, tougher on Peter than on Andrew but downright punitive with the Pharisees. Without requisite he delivered demoniacs and but rebuked his followers when they showed little or no faith.

Sometimes he did this, and other times he did that. In a word, he was unpredictable.

To debate or not to debate, that is often the question. Solomon's advice is sometimes do and at other times, don't. For example . . .

One day I approached an orthodontically challenged hippie-traveller, named "Feather," and asked him what he thought about Jesus. *"I don't believe in any of that Jesus stuff,"* he said with some snide behind it. *"Religion is just made up by people who want to control everybody else."*

A dozen verses and smart comebacks that I had used many times before ran through my mind. My Bible knowledge and trove of witnessing witticisms notwithstanding, after a brief pause I said, *"I know what you mean. From the outside it can sure seem that way."* I paused again and then decided to change the subject to the weather or something. It just seemed like the best thing to do at the time.

Later that week in our city's skid row I was out inviting people to our street service when I approached "Raymond" who was sitting in his wheelchair on the sidewalk out in front of his slum hotel. He spoke first, *"What's this religious propaganda you're spouting?"* Before I could respond he went into a tirade, spewing his objections to Christianity, as he understood it. He carried not only a colon-full of animosity about life in general, but a head-full of misinformation about Jesus.

In that case I felt led to kindly push back on a couple of his aberrant ideas while making every effort to exude as much love and humble compassion as I could. We ended up "debating" for an hour or so, became fairly well acquainted with each other, then parted on surprisingly good terms. My arguments for faith didn't convince him, but he thanked me for the effort and for just taking the time to converse.

A one-size-fits-all approach to sharing Jesus is lazy and immature. There is no one-trick evangelistic method. Sometimes, we should go ahead and answer people's objections and sometimes we shouldn't.

Have you noticed that Jesus asked a lot of questions? It's odd when you think about it, God asking questions, as though he didn't already know the answers! All the more do we have to ask questions in order to find out where people are coming from. Our goal to introduce them to Jesus notwithstanding, it's simply interesting to learn about someone's way of looking at the world and its Maker. We have to take time to learn about them without being in such a light-speed rush to download all our brilliant presentations of spiritual realities.

Believe me, I know how to put a preach on, and when it seems like the thing to do at the time, I do. But sometimes just listening and saying very little is a better way to go. Sometimes it might be advisable to speak to a sinful behavior and other times not so much. Just because something is true doesn't mean we need to say it up front. For instance if I'm a little overweight, and without being invited, you break into offering me dieting advice you might not get very far without me tuning you out mid-recipe.

Being the one Christian they've ever talked with that didn't go into a fevered sales pitch might just be the best thing we can do for this particular God-loved soul at the time. Being "ready with an answer to the hope that we have" does not necessarily mean that we have to give a reason *every time.* We should be ready to give an answer and ready not to.

I know, a memorized pre-scripted spiel would be an easier route to take. But that's not always the way of the Spirit of wisdom. I've found that he is available, even anxious, to whisper directions if we'll slow down long enough to listen.

We have to stop to consider what's going on inside this person, what sort of relationship we have with them, and what the Spirit wants us to say through us at *this time* with *this person* on *this day.*

It was "the lost" that Jesus came all the way here to seek and to save.[87] It is wise to acknowledge that there's more than one brand of "lostness." Some drivers get caught up in the scenery and don't even know they're lost. Others know they're lost but try to figure it out without consulting a map or GPS. Then there are those who know they need help to get un-lost. Each one will require a different approach.

By the way, if the concept of "lost" is off-putting to you, go with "missing," as in those whom Jim Hendersen calls, "the people Jesus misses most!"[88]

To their credit, Joshua's scouts stayed in the moment, heard Rahab's cry for help, listened to the Spirit and gave her the good news of a better destiny. They willingly stepped outside the box of their preconceived notions of what the day would bring. In the same way, it's important that we be "cemented in flexibility" and proceed in showing and sharing God's love in creative ways.

Will we make mistakes along the way? Of course. Sometimes we will when we shouldn't and won't when we should. We can only do the best we can at the moment and pray that our blunders are small and seldom.

"What do I do, Lord?"

"*Sometimes do this,*" saith the Lord, "*and sometimes do that. Oh, and remember that I'm the Savior!*"

The "Jesus Bus"

> "Who the hell are you, God's dean of admissions?"
> — ANNE LAMOTT

> "We need to love people who don't yet know Jesus, not be mad at them for not believing the right things."
> — JIM HENDERSON

As far as the narrative goes, Joshua's scouts didn't see the need to engage in a debate with Rahab about the disparity between her god and theirs. She already seemed to recognize the superiority of their faith to hers. She had heard stories about their God and was convinced they were true. She called Yahweh by name, acknowledged him as Creator, and feared him as righteous Judge (Joshua 2:9-11).

Billions of people on the planet today believe in a different god, with a different nature, personality, and agenda. How do we introduce them to the Jesus we love?

Do all roads lead to God? No, decidedly not. The Bible is clear on that point. That said, God is willing to drive down any road to reach those he loves. Allow me a metaphor.

They don't have one bus line that goes directly from my house to AT&T Park where the San Francisco Giants play. I have to ride one bus in the general direction of the stadium and transfer to another, which drops me off right in front of the ballpark.

There are "buses" that, spiritually speaking, travel in the general direction of the one true God. They won't take people *all the way* there, but they might deposit them closer to him than when they began their trip.

Jesus is the only way to the Father but there are a number of *ways to Jesus*. As earlier indicated, *creation, conscience, culture, crises* and even some aspects of *creeds* (religion) are like those buses that lead people to the *"Jesus Bus!"* They can serve as *vehicles* that can bring them to *The Vehicle* that brings them to God. Yes, it is necessary for devotees of other religions to "transfer" from their *former way* to *The Way* in order to get *all the way* to the Father. What the process of *transfer* looks like is so far above my pay grade that I can only speculate.

Since all truth is God's truth, wherever it's found, his invitations get incorporated into less than accurate creeds. He's working behind the scenes even in the world's religions. While it's true that religious systems of all stripes can represent people's attempts to *evade the truth*, they may also reflect their sincere attempts to *find it*.

That being said, we might begin by looking for common ground with people of other faiths on which to build, and locate "traces of truth" in their systems rather than expending all our energy tearing down the fallacies of their beliefs. Yes, there are many disparities between the religions and the way of Jesus, but it occurs to me to give more attention to the things about which we agree and build on that narrative. The most effective witnesses acknowledge the shared narrative with other spiritual views and build on top of it.

Veteran missionary to India, E. Stanley Jones wrote: "Any truth, any goodness, or any beauty found in other cultures is a ray of 'the light which lights every man that comes into the world.' Christ has been there before us, though unrecognized and unknown." He went on to say, "When I come to another civilization I know in my heart of hearts that Christ is not the enemy but the preserver of any fine trait or tendency or teaching in that civilization."[89]

Jesus is a highly esteemed personality even in our pluralistic culture. Since he's the most fetching Person who ever lived it's no surprise that people are attracted to him. Thus he is a good point of entry into most conversations with pre-christians. Though they might have a bunch of misconceptions about him, instead of rushing to correct all those you might celebrate their attraction and employ it as a springboard into telling them what you know to be true about him and why you love him so much.

In comparing religions, rather than simply trying to prove the others wrong, sometimes it's best to tell the truth about Jesus and let the truth speak for itself. When they hear it, the differences may become obvious.

The world's religions not only *hide*, but *reveal* certain aspects of the truth about the true God. Out of the billion Hindus in India many are bound to be true God-seekers. Having only been exposed to their own pantheon of gods, steeped in the religious culture of their land, and worshipping according to the light they have, isn't it possible that with a little help they can find their way onto the *Jesus Bus?*

I've seen a number of seekers that realized that the bus they were riding was so toxic that they jumped off before they crashed and burned. Terrified and bruised, they accepted an invitation to ride the *Jesus Bus*. They were scared all the way onto the *right bus* going the *right way* to the *right place.* In such case, even a particularly "bad bus" played a role in inadvertently "delivering" riders to the *Jesus Bus!*

The world's religions are absolutely not all saying the same thing about God or about how to get into relationship with him. To say otherwise is false tolerance and sloppy thinking. Still I contend that most religions contain enough similarities with the truth of Scripture and that some of their adherents are actually looking for God.

Someone said that as the sun rises in the East it shines through window after window of a house, each window representing the world's religions. They claimed that Buddha and Mohammed and Jesus were windows to let in the light in their own way. But Jesus is not a window. He is the sun shining into those other widows. He is the light itself.

If this is true then it means that we should be on the lookout for people whose bus has taken them *part way* to God. There are probably more people involved in alternative spiritualities than we realize who are *"not far from the kingdom of God."*[90] Since God has been communicating with them before we arrived it behooves us to take an interest in what he's been saying before we launch into our *torrent of talk*. Knowing that they are travelling in the general direction of The Way, might help us frame our dialog about what we've found in Jesus and might clue us in to the best way to invite them to ride his bus.

Our buses here in San Francisco clearly display their bus line numbers and destinations on the front of each one. In addition, most bus stops are equipped with a list of the stops along that particular route. If that's not enough, each stop has an automated readout that tells those waiting how long their wait will be, to say nothing of the iPhone app that does everything but lift them onto the bus when it arrives.

I spent some time in a small town in Mexico whose bus system, by comparison, left quite a bit to be desired, especially if your Spanish is weak and you're not familiar with the street names. Instead of a scrolling electronic sign on the front, each bus carries a thunder-throated man whose job is to stand on the bottom step in the wide-open doorway and holler to those waiting at each stop where the bus was headed. "DESTINO CALLE ZOCALO!" he bellows at the top of his lungs while clutching the handrail and leaning far outside the door. It's pretty entertaining actually. What their system lacked in automation it made up in ingenuity. Plus, it gave people jobs who might not otherwise have been employable.

We *Jesus Bus* riders have a job similar to the bus-line-caller, beckoning those waiting alongside the road at each and every stop: "DESTINATION: GOD! THE RIDE IS FREE. YOUR FARE WAS PAID. COME ABOARD! WELCOME TO THE JESUS BUS!"

Now let's return to Rahab's saving encounter with God. We've established that she had a "supernaturally installed wonder" and that the scouts accidentally "evangelized" her. But at the end of the day neither of these saved her from Jericho's destruction. There was something *she* had to do in order to access God's saving mercy.

Rahab's Redemptive Red Rope

> *"Sharing faith is not like teaching a class on the fundamentals. It's more like riding on a train with our hand out to give people running alongside a chance to come aboard."*
> — **Anonymous**

> *Now the men had said to her, "This oath you made us swear will not be binding on us unless, when we enter the land, you have tied this scarlet cord in the window through which you let us down, and unless you have brought your father and mother, your brothers and all your family into your house."*
> — **Joshua 2:17-18**

Most Bible teachers affirm that the "scarlet cord" calls to mind the crimson blood of Jesus. Rahab's *redemptive red rope* might be seen as the Jericho version of the Jewish Passover. In order to escape God's judgment on Egyptians, they painted the blood of the sacrificial lamb on their doorposts. Like the Jews in Egypt, Rahab and her family eluded judgment by displaying the crimson emblem of the cross in her window.

There's every indication that the red rope by which the scouts climbed down was the very same one that Rahab dangled out her window and eventually used as her exit strategy from judgment. The implication is clear. The same red rope rescues both the lowly prostitute and the highly trusted recon scout. Jesus' blood saves anyone willing to take hold of it!

There's a ministry in India that rescues and rehabilitates survivors of sexual slavery, called "Rahab's Rope." The founder says: "The rope in the story represents Rahab's rescue both physically and spiritually, and there is a high probability that Rahab made the rope herself. Our hope is that, just as the rope that Rahab made represents her rescue, the skills taught to the women at our women's centers will represent their physical and spiritual rescue as well."

The British Royal Navy used to weave a scarlet thread throughout all their rope. No matter where you cut it, this red thread could be seen and the rope identified as British made. Figuratively, you might say that God wove a scarlet thread—the story of sacrifice—to run throughout the entire Bible and that wherever you open it you'll find Jesus' sacrificial blood represented. You see the thread in the Mosaic sacrificial system, in the prophets' predictions, in Jesus' own prophecies in the gospel narratives, in the preaching of the Apostles, in their epistles, and even in the book of Revelation. If there's a prominent theme throughout God's Book, it's Jesus' bloody sacrifice.

It would be a stretch to claim that the scouts fully understood that the red rope signified Rahab's salvation from judgment. But being immersed in the Passover story and the miles of scarlet thread woven into the tabernacle and priests' vestments, it's conceivable that they inadvertently chose the red rope to make a creative—if not oblique—reference to her deliverance by sacrifice.

Jesus frequently illuminated his message by referring to farmers' seeds, shepherds' sheep, and vinedressers' vines. You might say that the scouts subconsciously used the red rope to "preach the gospel" to Rahab. In like fashion, we should be keen to read the clues that the Spirit places in front of us and creatively employ them in sharing the salvation story.

The scouts didn't have time to tell the whole story about sacrificing lambs and painting doorposts. Opportunities for unpacking the redemption story would come later. For the moment, a red rope would have to do. Similarly, many of our gospel-telling opportunities are time-sensitive and require a resourceful use of whatever object or metaphor that presents itself.

Don't go down with the wall! Drape this blood-stained rope from your window and climb into God's saving arms!

Though the Bible doesn't explicitly state it, I imagine Rahab and her family scaling down the red rope to safety on their way to a new life among the people of God. She trusted the integrity of the rope and the promise of the witnesses that it would hold. Similarly, you and I trust the flawless and sufficiently sturdy sacrifice of Jesus to carry the weight of our sins and deliver us to the Father's arms.

The rope spanned the distance between Jericho and Judaism. One end hung from Rahab's window and the other touched down on the land of the free. Job yearned out loud for a Jesus-like mediator between him and God, one "who might lay his hand on us both," someone to span the gap between them.[91] Paul, who had a clearer New Testament picture of the rope that redeems, claimed that Jesus is that very "mediator between God and mankind." [92]

From top to bottom, every inch of the redemptive rope is the color red. Christ's blood isn't a *piece* of the saving story; it's the *whole* story! He didn't pay the first payment and expect us to come up with the rest.

What can wash away my sin?
Nothing but the blood of Jesus!

They made no strenuous climb from Rahab's window to safety outside Jericho's wall. Gravity did what it does and all they had to do was hold on with relaxed grip (the grip whose New Testament name is "faith").

"It is easy to say we believe a rope to be strong and sound as long as we are merely using it to wrap a box," wrote C.S. Lewis. "But suppose you had to hang by that rope over a precipice. You would really want to first discover how trustworthy that rope was." Rahab's is a trustworthy rope. It's strong enough to hold all humanity at one time, and deliver us to safety. "He is the atoning sacrifice for our sins, and not only for ours but also for the sins of the whole world."[93]

Therefore, witnesses and witness-ees alike are afflicted with the same condition that requires the same prescription. The Jesus that we offer to others is the same Jesus that we need for ourselves. Put in terms of the Rahab narrative, we require and rely on the same redemptive rope that we offer to others.

As I read it, the rope Rahab draped out her window and used to scale down Jericho's wall was the very same red rope that the scouts put to use for their escape some days before. The rope was meant for both Jewish scouts and pagan prostitutes; for insiders and outsiders.

As the scouts were in no way superior to the town prostitute, we have a common need of redemption with the people we attempt to bring to Jesus. We're the same as the *lostest* of the lost—trashed by our sin and yet treasured by the Savior. We can only share as much of Jesus as we're clutching onto for ourselves. Thus, our message is: "Join us at the cross!"

Remember it's the rope that saves, not how well we comprehend it. We don't have to grasp it perfectly, to climb down the rope or to encourage others to join us. Its strength is bound up in what it is, not in how well we understand it or how well we communicate it to others. As with any of Jesus' miracles—walking on water, turning water to wine, or healing the blind—his miracle of salvation is as high above our thoughts "as the heavens are above the earth."[94]

It's not for us to fortify the rope, just trust the rope and preach the rope and nothing but the rope so help us God!

As most people who come to Jesus, Rahab first believed *about* God from what she had heard and then she came to believe *in* him. She learned to trust the God she had formerly only feared. She progressed from terror of his judgment to trust in his mercy.

It's not our dazzling presentations or fetching personalities that saves people. It takes a Savior to do that. The Bible's most fruitful evangelizer "boasted" in the redemptive red rope (Galatians 6:14) and trusted its power to save (Romans 1:16). His confidence in the saving blood of Jesus was such that he could say:

> *"I didn't try to impress you with polished speeches and the latest philosophy. I deliberately kept it plain and simple: first Jesus and who he is; then Jesus and what he did—Jesus crucified."*
> — **1 Corinthians 2:2 (The Message)**

PART FOUR

Befriending the Prostituted

> *"I used to think that to be Christlike meant to be alienated and put off by the sin of others. But it's quite the opposite. Refusing to be alienated and put of by the sin of others is what allows me to be Christlike."*
> — **BRANT HANSEN**

The very first "convert" in the Promised Land was no moral pillar of the community but an idolatrous prostitute! If that doesn't give us a glimpse of God's wide and wooly welcome, I don't know what does. Rachel Held Evans said, "The Gospel isn't offensive for whom it leaves out but for who it lets in!"

I'm sure glad he let *me* in.

Surely by design, Matthew includes only three of the many women in his genealogy of Jesus. Tamar, who played the harlot;[95] Bathsheba, who slept with a married king;[96] and the subject of our study, Rahab the Jerichoan prostitute.

I'm pretty sure that Joshua's advance men didn't go to Rahab's house to buy sex. They probably just thought they'd blend in better there. With all the male foot traffic in and out of her place, two more would raise no immediate suspicion within the community.

Innocent motives notwithstanding, what would the guys back at the camp think when they told them where they had held up? What would the elders of the people say about their choice of accommodations? Worse, what would the wife think? Or Joshua?! I'm sure he didn't send them out with orders to hide in a brothel. That said, it doesn't seem like they were too worried about appearances. They needed Rahab for shelter as much as she needed them for salvation.

Remember, Jesus lived a scandalously loving life, even befriending prostitutes and other misfits. He constantly violated obvious social taboos, and though people groused about it, he either blew them off or used their objections as a teaching moment to help get people unstuck from stigmas. He told his critics that he was in the hunt for the *sick* instead of the strong and that his gospel was most effective with the desperate, like the poor and prostituted. If we're trying to be like Jesus, Rahab-reaching has to be in the top ten of our list of life purposes.

Remember the "sinful woman" who wet Jesus' feet with her tears, wiped them with her hair, kissed them, and anointed them with perfume? Can you imagine this happening to your pastor at a church potluck? Right in front of the potato salad a woman dressed like a prostitute comes in and starts kissing his feet! Not so good for job security I'd say. The first question would be, "How do you know this woman?" The second, "How *well* do you know her?"

Rather than recoil, Jesus rebuked the host for what he was thinking, and then turned to her and said, "Your sins are forgiven. Your faith has saved you. Go in peace." (Luke 7:48-50) That's our Rahab-loving Jesus!

John Burke said: *"If you owned a Rembrandt covered in mud, you wouldn't focus on the mud or treat it like mud. Your primary concern would not be the mud at all, though it would need to be removed. You'd be ecstatic to have something so valuable in your care. But if you tried to clean the painting by yourself, you might damage it. So you would careful bring this work of art to a master who could guide you and help you restore it to the condition originally intended. When people begin treating one another as God's masterpiece waiting to be revealed, God's grace grows in their lives and cleanses them... Do you see the mud or the masterpiece?"*

We can't very well reach *Rahabs* if we villainize them and let our *revulsion* for their lifestyle trump our *compassion* for them as fellow beloveds. Some "Christians" are quick to pull out their morality pistols and start firing away, but it's up to us to show more *instinctual empathy* than *moral aversion* for the least, the last, and the lost among us. We can't act like people disgust us and say that we love them at the same time. I've heard it said, "If we succeed in loving we succeed big; if we fail to love we fail completely."

Late one night Bramwell Booth, son of William Booth, the founder of the Salvation Army found his father pacing up and down the floor late at night. "What are you thinking about?" asked the son. "Ah, Bramwell," he replied with a tear, "I'm thinking about the people's sin. What will people do with their sin?"

The opposite of apathy is empathy. The term "apathy" doesn't mean that we don't *care,* it literally means that we don't *feel.* George Bernard Shaw said, "The worst sin towards our fellow creatures is not to hate them, but to be indifferent to them." Empathy, on the other hand, is to feel what others feel—to feel with them. "Empathy," says Joseph Aldrich, "is the ability to become a naturalized citizen of another person's world."

Dan Kimball asks, "Do we ever weep as Jesus did for those who reject him? Or do we weep only at the emotional solo that someone sings in a church meeting about how much we're loved?"

We have to remember that we're not the judges but the *witnesses.* The prostituted women that we meet in San Francisco's skid row are vacuous souls contained in emaciated bodies who are desperate for a fix and bear no resemblance to the high priced "escorts" you see in the movies. With the bulk of their available veins collapsed, we've seen them slumped on the sidewalk shooting up in their necks! We pray to see what Jesus sees, feel what he feels, and follow him into the lives of people who need him most.

I live four blocks away from the heart of the City's Castro District, world famous for its thriving LGBT community. Many of the things I see in my neighborhood make me feel terribly uncomfortable. The park across from my apartment is the gathering place for both the transgender and dike parades held annually on Gay Pride weekend. I admit that I'm repelled by it all, but my foremost instinct over the tens of thousands of confused *Rahabs* in my neighborhood is heartache. "You can't wash the feet of a dirty world," says Erwin McManis, "if you refuse to touch them."

I have some friends who run a safe house for trafficking survivors in the Pacific Northwest. They told me that in their town traffickers will allow their victims to attend church, knowing that "Christians" tend to keep them at arms length, and therefore present little chance of them being rescued!

Rahab's "walled city" is no safe haven but a prison. Our mandate is to invite her to a way out and the way into a better life. Though we're offended by her lifestyle, we know that she is a tangled up soul for whom Jesus bled, and for whom he continues to suffer the sorrow of unrequited love.

John Wesley described how he felt when approached by desperate beggars:

> "Through his dirt and rags I see one that has an immortal spirit, made to know and love and dwell with God to eternity: I honour him for his Creator's sake. I see through all his rags that he is purpled over with the blood of Christ and I love him for the sake of his Redeemer. The courtesy therefore which I feel and show toward him is a mixture of the honour and love which I bear to the offspring of God, the purchase of his Son's blood, and the candidate for immortality. This courtesy let us feel and show toward all."

If anything, Rahab represents the dehumanized, marginalized, and overlooked people in any society. In this final section we'll focus on reaching the Rahabs in our own context. These are folks who are invisible, or worse, untouchable. Yet, if we see them through the lens of Scripture, we might consider them some of the world's most reachable of souls.

Consider Jesus' repeated claim that "the first will be last and the last will be first." Among other things I take this to mean, "Reach out to the last first." It's not that he loves them most, but they're the most needy of love, so he begins there. It's not that he cares nothing for those who are at the head of society's line, but that he rushes first to the back of the line!

Just as a doctor focuses on his sick patients over the well, Jesus said he came for the sick who know they need him most. He was called to preach his gospel first to "the poor" (Luke 4:18). The rich and healthy need him as much as they do. They're just less aware of their need.

Though he loves all people equally, he may seem biased toward the world's neediest. But as Ron Sider points out, "equal concern for everyone requires special attention to specific people. In a family, loving parents do not provide equal tutorial time to a son struggling hard to scrape by with D's and a daughter easily making A's. Precisely in order to be 'impartial' and love both equally, they devote extra time to helping the needier child… (Good firefighters do not spend equal time at every house; they are 'partial' to homes on fire.)"[97]

If God puts the disadvantaged and disregarded at the head of the line, doesn't it follow that we should do the same?

Humanizing the Dehumanized

> *"Name one harlot who has ever been reclaimed by treating her as a harlot."*
> — **Anonymous**

> *"What if we looked at our world with pity and not with blame? What if we heard God's call to evangelize out of love instead of fear, hope instead of judgment? What if we saw sin for the complex mixture it is, grounded in wounds and unmet needs? In short, what would it mean to read our world with a hermeneutic of love?"*
> — **Elaine Heath**

We know very little about Rahab. We know she had a more than meager revelation of who God was and what he could do. We know that when she saw an opportunity for escape she jumped on it. We know that she cared enough about her family to appeal for their rescue along with her own. And, of course, we know that she was a prostitute.

Prostitution is seldom a woman's chosen profession. Most don't get into the business for the good pay and benefits. It's not as though anyone likes being mounted everyday by a string of sex-crazed strangers. Even those who do choose the life for whatever reason are degraded by the "work." Regardless of the motive, the effect is the same.

The prostituted are not regarded as the most valued members of society. They are valuable as a commodity to their handlers and customers, but only for financial gain or sexual indulgence. Everyone in Jericho knew who Rahab was but few "knew" her. They all saw her around town, but few "saw" her, at least not as a fellow citizen. Her patrons used her and her neighbors undoubtedly scorned her.

Prostitution is a dehumanizing path into which most in the trade are deceived or coerced. Selling one's body for survival is for the desperate, the last resort for the victims of bone-crushing poverty and social marginalization. She is simply human "merchandise" to the heartless broker and the soulless buyer.

Greed appeals to sex for sale
At her expense, it mirrors hell
A grave inside a human's mind
They lock the doors and close the blinds
A human life is thrown in a cage
Raped until death, then thrown away
Deeds in the dark the light reveals
And judgment comes when the blood is spilled

They even changed her name
They even changed her name
They even changed her name

This stanza and refrain from John Scott Young's haunting song, *Different Name*, conveys a fragment of the misery of a prostituted soul. Her pimp lives in luxury while she is "raped until death, then thrown away." Having already robbed her of dignity, to further isolate her and decimate any semblance of her God-given identity, he changes her name to something more exotic and something less—*hers*.

If he can get her to forget who she is, she'll be less apt to escape her hell and be more apt to continue as his low budget, low maintenance slave. As if branding an animal, some soulless traffickers tattoo their own names on the necks of their slaves so that whenever they look in the mirror, they won't forget who they belong to!

No one should ever be robbed of their name, along with it their unique identity and destiny. "By trying not to over-identify people with their difficult contexts and by calling friends by their actual names when possible," says Christopher Heuertz, (we) offer the hope that comes with affirming the distinctive and divine imprint of God in each person."[98]

The little we can gather from the narrative, the scouts seemed to treat Rahab as a fellow image-bearer of the divine. There's no hint of disrespect in their conversation with her. Thus began the reversal of the dehumanizing effect of her "profession."

Leapfrogging ahead fifteen hundred years or so, consider the Samaritan woman at the well a New Testament Rahab of a sort.[99] Though she was on the wrong side of every fence, Jesus treated her as fully human and wholly beloved. She was a woman, not a man; a Samaritan, not a Jew; and immoral, instead of moral. To the Jews, including his own disciples, she was an outsider in every respect. Add to that, some commentators suggest that the well at Sychar, like Rahab's house, was a place to pick up women. Jesus didn't care as much about her location on the social registry or her lifestyle as he cared about her as a person. And, as a result, like Rahab, she turned around to influence those around her and "many became believers" that day.[100]

Now, two thousand years later, millions of women and children are still trafficked into the trade by force, fraud, or coercion for which they pay all the dues and receive nothing back but a ravaged body and a tortured soul.

John says that some wicked people make merchandise of "the bodies and souls of (other) people."[101] It's not like we need the Bible to tell us that buying and selling humans is wrong, but sometimes God states the obvious because to some people it isn't so obvious. Just in case we were wondering, he commands such things as: "Don't have sex with animals or with relatives. Don't steal the only blanket a poor man has, or take your neighbor's wife, or sell your fellow human beings like you would a cow or a sack of wheat!"

There's no way to put a nice sheen on it. Bludgeoning the bodies of others and stealing their souls for nothing but money is a coldblooded insult to the Creator and the people he loves.

I tag along with some dreadlocked hippie Christian friends of mine to Golden Gate Park to bring pancakes and coffee to those who call the park "home" and to those passing through to other traveler enclaves and Rainbow Gatherings around the country. Most begin each day smoking pot, drinking alcohol, or shooting heroin and don't stop until they pass out or the night is done. Many of our friends are mentally disabled, emotionally shredded social exiles, all with an immense need to be loved.

Recently, like Joshua's scouts I was out doing recon in the eastern end of the park inviting to our circle anyone who looked like they could use a meal. I stopped to talk to "Wheels," a mid-twenties, park "frequent flyer" that we've known for a while whose preferred form of local travel is his skateboard—thus the moniker. It was well before noon and Wheels was already completely hammered on cheap wine, seesawing between grief and rage over his breakup with his girlfriend the night before. She had cheated on him and he couldn't decide who to kill, himself, her, or the guy who stole her away from him.

I sat next to him on the ground and listened to him rant for quite a while, trying to slip in a hopeful word or two every now and then. Unless the Spirit descends and sobers them in an instant—something I have seen—most attempts at formal gospeling at times like that are all but futile. As I settled into much more listening than lecturing, his inebriated state stacked on top of his emotional ordeal loosened his tongue and out poured one of the most nauseating childhood stories I've ever heard about how his father rented him and his twin sister out to men for drug money! Doesn't get much more soulless than that.[102]

People dehumanize one another in ways other than sexual exploitation—child and spousal abuse, racism, classism, and gender bias to name a few. Irrespective of color, status, or lifestyle everyone deserves to be treated with civility. And there's nothing more equalizing than the gospel and no one like the Maker of humans to humanize the dehumanized.

Rahabs of all sorts need friends—sincere, non-judgmental friends—a rare possession of the dehumanized, to be sure. "Othering" people and befriending them are contradictory behaviors. Friends don't refer to their friends as inanimate objects: *"Those gays, those homeless, those democrats..."*

Human warmth is not the norm for society's throwaways, whose ability to connect with others on a deep level is damaged. They're wrecked for authentic human connection altogether, which gives us all the more reason to be safe enough for them to give connection a try.

Is this not the very essence of good news bearing?

Re-earning Trust

"They usually only see the ways the bride acts in ways that doesn't honor the groom."
— **Dan Kimball**[103]

"**O**kay, Houston, we have a problem here!" The problem that the Apollo 13 crew had was technical, ours is *relational*. In both cases, unless solved, death is the unavoidable result.

Once upon a time most people trusted Christians, preachers, and churches. That time has pretty much passed as their trust has evaporated under the scorching heat of our hypocrisy. We live in an age of distrust and suspicion, especially when it comes to the Church and its spokespersons and it's mostly our fault.

This is one of our biggest obstacles in our attempts to offer Jesus to people—they don't trust us. And if they don't trust *the messenger* it's going to be a long dusty road for them to come to trust *the message*. When trust has not yet been established, lostness feels like wise skepticism and right thinking. Trust isn't handed over like a bagel with cream cheese in exchange for a couple bucks plus tax. It's earned. That's the rule.

Identifying as "Christian" makes us complicit in the debacles committed by other Christians in the world yesterday, today, and forever. Object to it all you want but our track record is entwined with everyone else who identifies as Christian. Sure, we've contributed mountains of good to the world but we've also dumped a lot of crap on it! And since the latter out-smells the former, that's what people think of when we treat them like projects and say with a smile, "Would you like to hear the Good News?" We've got a lot of work to do to re-earn their trust.

Surely, our case study, Rahab, had no innate trust in Jews or their religion in general, but at some point her interaction with the scouts convinced her that they were legit. Somehow they won her trust.

Going forward, Rahab went on to trust them beyond her rescue when she accepted their invitation to enter their community. It took a great deal of trust for her to join the Jewish community, marry into it, and start a family. You have to admit that it was quite a leap from her pagan prostitute's life to being grafted into Judaism.

They kept their word and earned her trust. Unfortunately, we're not exactly known for living up to our word. We have so often over-promised and under-delivered that they don't trust us, and sadly, to them, our Jesus is suspect as well.

"Christians are hard to tolerate;" says Bono, "I don't know how Jesus does it." And he's a Christian!

Everts and Schaupp cite "five significant shifts that tend to go on in postmodern folks as they come to faith."[104]

1. *From distrust to trust*
2. *From complacent to curious*
3. *From being closed to change to being open to it*
4. *From meandering to seeking*
5. *From one kingdom to the other*

I think they're on to something and highly recommend their book. It's highly unlikely, no matter how much we try to scrunch people's salvation process into one stage, for them to go from calloused to converted in one conversation. The question is, "How we can discern and then enter their stage of the journey and help them forward?"

I'd like to highlight just the first threshold—from distrust to trust. This is where it all begins. The value of authenticity, especially among postmoderns is hard to overrate. Once they start to significantly trust us, sharing the message of coming to Jesus really gains traction. But we can't very well expect people to trust our Christ if they're all gummed up with mistrust for his followers. We have to find ways to earn their trust back.

Does it bother you that when they think about Christians a lot of people see us as "angry, judgmental, right-wing finger-pointers with political agendas"?[105] You might not think this is a fair characterization; but it's a reputation that, by association, is ours. Maybe it's true that for every individual who earned the world's mistrust there are ten legitimate Christ followers who deserve a better rap. Problem is, it's harder to unlearn something wrong than to learn it right the first time. Helping our culture unlearn their notions about us and, more importantly, notions about Jesus, is an uphill battle.

You've probably seen the diagrams with the little man who walks across Jesus' cross to get to God. It's a great graphic, actually. But since mistrust for Christians and our churches has become its own chasm, a pre-chasm if you will, something often has to be done about bridging that before a person is even willing to hear about the sin chasm and trust the cross to save them.[106] And no amount of slick evangelistic techniques or impressive apologetics will span the gap that can only be corrected by trust.

Since bridges are built over time, and most of our evangelistic encounters are brief, how can we prove to people that we're worthy of their trust? We can't expect to overcome years of dashed trust to be remedied in one conversation. So, what's to be done?

First, while one-time witnessing encounters are good, we should be out "scouting" for more long-term relationship opportunities with people. It's best if we can walk with people over the long haul and demonstrate to them how a Christ-indwelt person acts. (And when we don't act that way, we're vulnerable enough to admit it and show them how we continue to access the redemptive rope!)

Second, when we're likely to see someone only once, like on the bus or at a seminar, we have to engage in such a way that when they walk away they can't in good conscience add our name to their list of "Jerks Who Call Themselves Christian." Let's give them no more reason to feel like a first time car buyer on a used car lot. They may not trust us yet per se, but at least, based on the one interaction, we've given them no more reasons to mistrust all Christians.

Third, we absolutely have to live with integrity 24/7. We never know who's watching, and believe me, they are watching. To put it bluntly, please don't try to witness *about* Christ if you're living a bad witness *for* him. Nobody's perfect, but there's a difference between hypocrisy and living repentantly.

Good witnesses are safe people with a dangerous message. We're *safe* because we're real and genuinely care about what's best for people. The message, on the other hand, is *dangerous* because when Jesus moves in he takes over. He knocks down the walls and replaces all the furniture. Receiving him is dangerous and rejecting him is even more so.

Some people begin their evangelistic interactions by pointing out what's wrong with their victims. I prefer, if they don't trust me yet, to start somewhere else. It's not that I'm afraid to share the bad news (of sin and judgment), which makes the good news (of salvation) necessary. It's that I suspect they'll be less apt to hear the bad news from someone they don't trust.

When a new acquaintance tells you how hammered they got over the weekend and woke up next to someone they don't remember meeting, though your sin-o-meter is triggered and you're tempted to quote Ezekiel chapter and verse, unless absolutely prompted by the Spirit, don't. Yes, speaking the truth in love is a thing, but even Jesus resisted the temptation to tell people everything he knew.

My general rule of thumb is to convey the radical cost of accepting or rejecting the gospel at a level commensurate with the trust I've built with someone. Otherwise it feels like I'm shouting at them from across the chasm to come over to our side. Once they trust me they'll be more apt to let me come close enough to take them by the hand and lead them over the bridge.

Rahab's trust in the scouts factored into her confidence in the redemptive red rope. I suspect it had something to do with their mutual vulnerability. When they met, Rahab, as well as the scouts, were desperate and in danger. They trusted her to hide them and she trusted them to return for her and her family. Vulnerability and mutual trust are at the foundation of any good friendship.

Mutualizing the Marginalized

> *"If you want to go fast, go alone. If you want to go far, go together."*
> — **AN AFRICAN PROVERB**

After her rescue, Joshua took Rahab and her family into their community (Joshua 6:25). They didn't promise her "forty acres and a mule" and kick her to the curb with a handshake and a friendly farewell. They had the audacity to relate to this pagan prostitute as a neighbor, part of their circle—so much so that she married one of their men and the rest is history.

Rahabs are untouchables who have been pushed out to the margins of society and been refused citizenship in the center with the rest and the "best" of us. Remember, it's a "friendship" quest into which God has invited us. Neil Cole said, "The Gospel flies best on the wings of relationships."

Friendship is by definition a mutual arrangement, a two-way street. Dr. Martin Luther King spoke of us all being bound up in an "inescapable web of mutuality." They called Jesus a "friend of sinners,"[107] which, for my money, implies more than that he was nice to bad people. He valued their friendship as much as they did his. Even those individuals that some people considered the dregs of his day must have, in some way, brought something of value to the relationship.

From a Rahab-like woman of notorious reputation Jesus asked, "Will you give me a drink?"[108] He was the least "needy" person who ever lived, and yet he opens the conversation with admitting a need. At face value, the woman had nothing to offer the Son of God, and yet he humbled himself and asked for her help. He was ready to dispense unlimited "living water," yet he approached her with his own need for the kind of water she had at her disposal. That's mutuality.

If that's the case with the eternal Son of God, how much more should we expect to benefit from calibrating how we befriend people outside our comfort zones of commonality and risk getting near people who are unlike us?

The way I read it Jesus was the sinner's friend even before the sinner converted to sainthood. That is, while his goal was to gain full access to sinners' hearts, he befriended them before they turned over the keys. Though, to fully enjoy the benefits of his friendship (i.e. to be saved) people must repent, he didn't wait for them to convert in order to be their friend. I think the same goes for us on our quest with him. People shouldn't have to come to faith before they can be our friends.

When Richard Nixon resigned and held up in isolation no one visited him for fear of sullying their reputation, no one except Chuck Colson who risked the trip many times. When asked about it later he said, "To let Mr. Nixon know that someone loved him."

I have a bunch of drug-doing—as well as a few drug-dealing—friends. "Mercedes," for instance, a vendor of illegal substances, has for years come and listened to us preach in the Tenderloin and sometimes even helps hand out food and clothing. She's our friend, and I think she would say the relationship is reciprocal. "Tommy" and "Eddy" and "Sapphire" sell all manner of illicit inebriants in Golden Gate Park. Our decided disapproval of their chosen profession notwithstanding, our friendship with them is genuine and mutual.

I want these friends of mine to fully come to Jesus and find a more legitimate line of work, but until then we're still friends. Of course, if and when they turn from their own way to turn to Jesus, our level of mutual trust and common bond would improve exponentially. That's our hope, but in the meantime, I hope to always consider them friends.

If there's one thing I've experienced in the last few years in San Francisco it's how socially marginalized friends enrich my life as much as I hope to enrich theirs. I genuinely enjoy the company of people outside my cultural comfort zone and I think they—well, most of them—would say the same about me.

As I said before, I propose no "friendship evangelism" model. "Befriending someone merely so you can tell them the gospel is a form of manipulation and a violation of trust," says Christopher Heuertz. "Some of our approaches to conversion have earned the mistrust of the very people we want to reach."[109] Treat people as people, not like evangelistic targets. Nobody likes to be targeted.

We're conditioned to make friends with those with whom we have the most in common. The weakness of that strategy is our criteria for commonality, which is often as shallow and incidental as socioeconomic, ethnic, and external appearance considerations. We have to look beneath exterior casing and financial portfolio factors, and explore into deeper parts where you'll find the divine imprint. This is our common bond.

James gives us a good place to begin forming mutually beneficial relationships *"Be quick to listen and slow to speak."* (James 1:19) We can't very well make friends with people when we do all the talking and all the giving and they do all the listening and all the receiving. One of the chief reasons we God-experts don't reach many *Rahabs*, or anyone else for that matter, is we insist on being the sole dispensaries of goodness and truth as though no one else on earth has anything to contribute to us. We assume that a not-yet-christian can't possibly know anything that we need to know or have anything that we need to have. If there's anything that keeps *Rahabs* from Christ, it's patronizing spiritual experts.

Again I quote Heuertz: "A focus on friendship [with the poor] rearranges our assumptions. What if the resources they have also meet our needs? What if Jesus is already present in ways that will minister to us? What if in sharing life together as friends we all move closer to Jesus' heart? . . . [Friendship] is an opportunity for all of us to be enveloped in God's grace and mercy."[110]

Outer Circle Christians

"This man welcomes sinners and eats with them."
— Luke **15:2**

Our story's main character was no high society standout in Jericho. Rahab probably *stood out*, but not in the way in which one aspires. Nor was she a likely candidate for the Proper Ladies' Tea Association or voted Woman of the Year—woman of the night maybe, but that's another thing.

I'm intrigued that the scouts went to her door rather than to a more respected member of the community. I believe that one of the Spirit's lessons in this story is that God begins in a different place and with different people than we would. He embarks on his quest to find friends on the margins, the outermost circle of society, the poor, downtrodden, and vulnerable.

Not everyone is called specifically to the most marginalized but after reading both testaments I have to conclude that every true follower of Jesus is called to *care about* and even *care for* the poor in some way.

I first realized that God expected me to befriend a lot more individuals of meager resource when in a worship service at a faith-based drug rehab facility for men, a couple dozen careworn residents were crammed into a small, poorly ventilated room, each battling their own demons. These men, whose addictions had kicked them to the curb, sleep in bunk beds, shower in decrepit shared stalls, and eat whatever the center can afford that month.

The service consisted of worship songs, testimonies about how God was untangling them from inebriants, and a sermon that some might consider more sweat than substance. It was during the closing song that I heard the words in my mind, *"These are your people,"* which on reflection indicated that my new circle of friends were going to be the desperate, the defeated, and diseased. Both men and women Rahabs were about to become my primary mission field.

As I indicted before, God doesn't specifically assign everyone to this same socioeconomic demographic, lest the entire middle and upper class sinners be passed over for salvation. That said, I can't sufficiently convey the honor of serving those less advantaged than yourself, or how fertile the heart soil is among people of meager means. I'll come back to that thought later.

I spend quite a bit of time with some amazing young urban missionaries in San Francisco that call themselves "The Outer Circle." They intentionally seek out and befriend people on society's ragged edge. Their motto is: *"To invite the lonely, the outcast, and the wanderer into restoration of their entire beings by drawing them to Christ, giving them what we have, bringing them into community, and being their friends."*

Most of our friends are addicts, slightly-to-severely mentally ill folk, and socially awkward individuals that most churchgoers wouldn't automatically choose to sit next to in their worship service.

"Inner Circle" is how we describe any elite few in an organization. Sometimes we use it to describe the three disciples closest to Jesus (Peter, James, and John), who were given special opportunities to be in the room when Jesus did something big like raise the dead or cast out of someone a particularly pesky demon.

Jesus, it seems, worked hard to teach his *inner circle* to care about *outer circle* people. He wanted their perimeter to be porous and penetrable in order to include castoffs. He was adamant that their insider sphere was not to become a barrier (as in a Jericho wall) between them and those who needed them most.

For the spiritual experts of his time, Jesus' welcome mat was way too wide. They didn't approve of the people he welcomed, how they looked, where they were from, or how they worshipped. Judaism's self-appointed *Inner Circle* wasn't the least bit interested in touching, let alone reaching, outer circlers. They were way too busy judging them to make friends with them. It's hard to give people a hand up *and* push down on them at the same time!

Inner Circlers tend to become enamored with their special status and move furthest away from the least desirable souls. Two of the disciples wanted special seats in the future kingdom, so they put in a request to incinerate members of the Samaritan cult. Not exactly what Jesus, the outer-circle-seeking-Savior had in mind when he told them to preach "good news"!

As God's special forces, they requested that he appoint them as generals in his kingdom to rule over all the lessers and undesirables. That's why they couldn't understand why he ate with LGBTs and lazy drug addicted homeless people—oops—I mean "sinners and tax collectors."

The Friendmaker gives special attention to those on society's margins. He doesn't just welcome them into the flock, but searches them out and carries his hobbled lambs back home.

"Yeah, but isn't it their fault that they can't walk? They ran off and tried to live without the shepherd, so shouldn't he make them walk home? I mean, no one held them down and pumped drugs into their veins. They're poor because they won't work. If they're gay they chose to be gay." (Well, maybe or maybe not. I don't know, I'm just repeating what I've heard people say.)

But do you actually think Jesus even cares how people got in their pit? Does it even matter whether they were pushed in or they jumped in? Did they hobble themselves by bad behavior or were they hobbled by others? What's the difference? They're hobbled and need someone to befriend them and carry them back home.

This brings to mind Richard Stearns' paraphrase of the well-known parable of Jesus: *For I was hungry, while you had all you needed. I was thirsty, but you drank bottled water. I was a stranger, and you wanted me deported. I needed clothes, but you needed more clothes. I was sick, and you pointed out the behaviors that led to my sickness. I was in prison, and you said I was getting what I deserved.*[111]

How did Rahab begin her life as a prostitute? Was she coerced or deceived into it? Or was her economic situation so dire that it was her only way to survive? Is it possible that she weighed her options and chose the work for its financial and fringe benefits? What's it matter how she got there? That's where she was when the scouts turned up at her door and, thank God that they did!

Jesus told three parables in succession about how God finds and recovers lost people in Luke 15. All three—the wandering sheep, the wayward son, and the missing coin—represent damaged, derelict, Rahab-like "outer circle" souls that need to find their way back home. Of the three, the lost coin parable[112] is the least familiar to most people and yet it contains some key components about our complicity with the Lord in his quest for friends.

It begins with a woman who misplaces one of her ten silver coins. I invite you to think of God as a collector of priceless coins--i.e., people stamped with his image and in his estimation, precious. Somehow, we're not told by what means the coin gets lost. Though it retains its intrinsic value, while lying in the dust out of circulation so to speak, the lost coin does no one any good. Its worth is indisputable but until it's found and restored to the woman it benefits no one. Its value can only be realized in the hands of its owner.

Similarly, Rahabs, though layered over with dust, shoved in a corner somewhere and unnoticed by most, are to the Lord, priceless gems stamped indelibly with his image. They must be found and brought home to realize their purpose. That's where *we* fit in…

The woman "lights a lamp" and begins her search. I think she's a picture of the Church who can only see in the dark, where her treasured coin lays in obscurity, by lighting a lamp. This reminds us how much we need the Holy Spirit to help us find trashed yet treasured people and empower us to bring them back to their rightful Owner.

Over time we Christians suffer from a sort of spiritual macular degeneration. We fail to *see* the people around us very well, especially outer circle people, Rahabs whom we deem the least of the lost. We're both lost. They don't know how to find God and we don't know how to find them. We need the Spirit to shed his light onto their hiding places, their walled Jerichos, so we can bring them home.

So she lights a lamp, but the lamp alone won't find her hidden coin. Like her, we play a crucial part, to sweep the dust out of every corner of the house and "search carefully" for what is lost.

She is determined to find what was mislaid and embarks on a meticulous quest for it. In contrast to the woman in the parable, we are far too casual about searching for and lifting lost people out of the dust. Though we can't save anyone, the Spirit can and will light the way so we can do the work of finding and returning them to Jesus who does all the necessary saving.

She suffered the loss of something priceless to her. Since she represents the Church, this is a message to us that those who remain lost to God are also lost to us and we suffer the loss along with him. Each treasured soul that is MIA is not only lost to heaven but missing from our spiritual family here on earth. Whether you think of them as Rahabs or silver coins, every person possesses enormous value to us as well as to God, and we're obligated[113] to find all lost coins within the reach of our influence and bring them home.

The menial task of *sweeping* is never beneath Outer Circle saints, whose privilege it is to don our work clothes and sweep till we uncover the coins, dirty yet dear to the Lord and to us. When back in his possession, he cleans and polishes each one till his stamped-on image is restored.

Jesus says that she sweeps and carefully searches "until she finds it." She's relentless in her search. She won't give up until she finds what she's looking for. In our search for lost souls, I believe we tend to give up too soon. We don't sweep and search with the same sort of persistence as the woman in the parable. Unaware that some sin-obscured precious soul lies near, we often make a trifling effort and call it a day—"No coins here!"

Outer Circlers, on the other had, see lost Rahabs and lost coins that others don't and are willing to search where others won't until they find them. It is their most sublime joy to join God in his passionate pursuit of people. If he doesn't give up, neither will they.

Speaking of sublime joy, the woman throws a party with her friends and neighbors and says, "Rejoice with me; I have found my lost coin!" This corresponds to the best party ever, the raucous celebration among the Father, Son, and Spirit, along with the angels and all saved souls in heaven and on earth! What could be more sublime than finding a human lost to God (and to us) and bringing them home?

Please, Lord, send us today to the ones that no one else wants.

Squeezing Camels

> *"Again I tell you, it is easier for a camel to go through the eye of a needle than for someone who is rich to enter the kingdom of God."*
> — **Matthew 19:24**

> *"The Gospel is only for the spiritually poor and especially for the actually poor."*
> — **Tim Keller**

Joshua—whose name means, "The Lord is Savior"—sent his two scouts to an unfamiliar place, where they *converted* a person with whom they had nothing socially, economically, or spiritually in common.

Jesus, whose name means the same in Greek as Joshua's does in Hebrew, and whose ministry—to lead as many into the Promised Land as possible—was parallel to his Old Covenant counterpart, sends his witnesses out two-by-two to Jerusalem and Judea as well as to the unfamiliar in Samaria and the ends of the earth.[114] As Rahab, a person of meager means but "spacious" in spirit was the scouts' first convert, so Jesus and his disciples went to the disparate yet desperate souls of their time bringing good news.

A friend asked me why I spend a majority of my outreaching efforts with the poor. "Spiritual" reasons first. Jesus had a thing for the poor, he told us that his gospel was to the poor, and I feel an unrelenting, and often unpleasant, pain in my heart for the destitute. I'm not trying to end world poverty. I just love the poor. Others smarter than me can address with the larger issues of systemic injustice, oppression, and deprivation. Especially in the inner city we need Nehemiah-like community development experts. John Stott used the illustration that the biblical blend of evangelism and social action are like the two pieces of scissors: if one part is absent, the scissors no longer function as scissors. For me, it begins with relationship. What I have to offer is friendship, and I think all of us can do that much.

But seeming nobler motives notwithstanding, I confess my not-so-spiritual reason for sharing Jesus more with the poor than with the rich—it's easier. The financially unfortunate tend more easily than the wealthy to fit through the needle-sized eye entry to the kingdom. They're more apt to realize their need for God than those privileged with economic security. The obstacles between them and God are fewer and the barrier more porous.

I claim no expertise on humpbacked, ruminant quadrupeds, but I know that, like rich people, they don't fit nicely through tiny openings. Whether we're talking about the kind of "needle" that you use to sew up your ripped jeans or an alleged opening in the Jerusalem wall called, "The Needle Gate," camels are simply too unwieldy to be shoved through the opening, especially when you factor in that extra bulge on his back!

The thing that makes Jesus' hyperbole that much more hyperbolic is the fact that these mammals of the open desert can survive long periods without food or drink only because they carry surplus resources saved up in their humps. The animal itself is already too big to traverse narrow spaces, but consider that awkward, albeit necessary protuberance on his back, and the metaphor just gets silly. It takes no graduate degree in zoology to reason that the bigger the hump, the more difficult it is to squeeze through a needle's eye!

A cursory scan of Wikipedia yields the fact that there are different classes of camels. Some hail from different locales, some are born in possession of one mere hump, and others are highborn—so to speak—entering the world with two. Like exceptionally wealthy folks, two-humpers lug around even more "savings" than their one-protuberance counterparts. I can't say that I've ever offered a camel a drink, let alone tried to shove one through a small opening, but my guess is that if he already carries either one or two hump-fulls, he's not apt to be terribly thirsty for more.

On the other hand, most of the seven billion people on our planet came into this world *humpless*. Not only so, but skinny to the point of concave. They carry no reserves with which to replenish themselves during lean days. For millions of poverty stricken souls, every day is a lean day.

It's no mystery then that the gospel is spreading the most rapidly in the planet's most impoverished places, where their wallet isn't too fat to fit through the kingdom's narrow gate. In many cases, when thirsty folks hear about an abundant source of living water, they rush toward it. What do they have to lose? Without any excess girth, they fit nicely through even the smallest needle's eye.

So, on a mere utilitarian level, why do we spend most of our time, energy, and money trying to shove the plumpest camels through the needle's eye when there are people "small enough" to slip through with room to spare? Why then do we often employ half the congregation to *push* and the other half to *pull* that one lone two-humper through the narrow gate? For heaven's sake, why?

I'm certainly *not* implying that Jesus' love was confined to the poor or that the wealthy were wide of his radar. One of his disciples (Matthew) was a person of means—ill-gotten means, notwithstanding. In fact, one of the few times we're told specifically that he did "love" a particular individual (besides John the Beloved), it's a rich young ruler, who walked away from Jesus because he was unwilling to unpack his hump.

I *am* saying that folks who are content with their lives "as is" don't tend to jump at the chance to give themselves to Jesus as readily as those with lesser means. Personal comfort often translates to spiritual complacency.

Not everyone lives under immanent threat like Rahab and her fellow citizens. The fact is, they're in every bit as much trouble as the Jerichoans; they just don't know it or refuse to acknowledge it. When Jesus said he didn't come for the healthy, he wasn't saying any such person actually exists! His point was that only those who admit they're sick go for help. Others live with a false sense of security, and in my experience these are the most difficult ones to bring to Jesus.

Of course the Spirit is hard at work sowing seed, so sometimes it's just a matter of waiting patiently until the bottom drops out, which it usually does at one point or another, in one way or another. Maybe it's a death in the family, a health problem, or a breakup; but for most people life doesn't roll along smoothly forever. And when things become less manageable they're more apt to call on the One with whom they've been avoiding eye contact.

It's not that his love doesn't reach the rich, but that the rich don't tend to *reach out* for his love. It only makes sense to devote more time, money, and effort on inviting people most likely to come to your party. Why, then, should we beat our heads against the wall begging those least likely to be interested in our simple gospel, when there are people whose life situation disposes them more naturally toward it?

There is one caveat worth mentioning when reaching out to the poor and disregarded. Whereas Rahab seemed receptive, even anxious, to leave her situation, there are many in life situations such as hers who need a firmer nudge to lean into God's love.

In one of his parables Jesus spoke about people who can be difficult to evangelize.[115] In it he said that those from the general population think they already have what they need (property and oxen) and have something better to do than attend God's banquet. So he invites in the "poor, crippled, blind, and lame." With only half the seats at the table filled he orders homeless vagabonds out on the "country lanes" to be invited. It seems that they would naturally feel unworthy of the master's generosity and too dirty to enter his house and they have to be compelled to accept his invitation. "Make them come in!" Jesus said.

Jesus prescribes neither coercion nor force but some people require a more insistent invitation. It's not so much that they need to be convinced about the beauty and bounty of the banquet, but these less advantaged folks simply can't conceive of the banquet master's generosity and wide welcome to such as them. They know how they look and smell, and feel unfit for such an elegant faire and such a generous host. They need a firmer nudge to come to the table.

When they do take us up on the Master's scandalous invitation, he treats them as guests of honor at the party. Joshua rescued Jericho's infamous prostitute from destruction and so much more. Even if Rahab was a bit tentative as she climbed down the redemptive red rope, she went on to enter the Jewish camp as a full-fledged member of the community, married one of its respected men, started a family, and joined the line of the Son of God!

If for no other reason, wouldn't it be better stewardship if we prioritized pursuing those of meager means? I'm not recommending that we neglect the rich. In fact, if you're middle class, you most likely work and live among people of your own socioeconomic status. So consider yourself blessed and share your faith with those who are in your closest sphere of influence. Gift them a Bible for Christmas and invite them to your Easter service. Love all your neighbors, whatever their station in life, and bloom where you're planted.

Granted, not everyone has a lot of easy access to disadvantaged people and would have to go out of their way to encounter the inadequately housed, fed, and clothed. For them it's a day trip to get out of their middle-class suburbs. If that's your privileged context, I urge you to venture outside your neighborhood once in a while and join God's friendship quest among the "humpless." Befriend some people who don't need to have their excess baggage surgically removed in order to fit through the narrow gate!

In this age of wiki-info about anything you'd ever want to know about anything under God's sun (or never want to know), we all know something about poverty. The problem is that most of us don't know any poor people. Mother Teresa said, "It is fashionable to talk *about* the poor… unfortunately it is not as fashionable to talk *to* the poor." Give it a try. You might like it.

You might be surprised by the Spirit's bothersome—yet winsome—tug on your heart for periodic, if not permanent, friendship-making among people unlike yourself. Make a legitimate experiment of it, but if after investigating you still feel called more exclusively to your own socioeconomic culture, then go for it. But even then, pray for and give generously to the poor and to those who serve them.

Rethinking Our Testimony

> *"Do not take a purse or bag or sandals... Stay there, eating and drinking whatever they give you..."*
> — LUKE **10:3**

Neediness is a great equalizer! The relationship between Joshua's two scouts and Rahab was mutually advantageous. They needed her as much as she needed them. Either would die without the other's help. They came to her for help and serendipitously ended up helping her in the process. She saved them from Jericho's police, and they saved her from Joshua's army. To reach *Rahabs,* we have to let *Rahabs* reach us. In our collaborative quest with God for friends, it's a give-and-take thing, a *symbiosis with sinners.*

One of the best things that ever happened to my testimony to needy people was to become needy myself. I have not historically done *needy* well at all. I like to be on top of things, but when things like divorce, cancer, and financial loss piled up on top of me, I learned how these misfortunes helped me connect with other unfortunates who live on the bottom of the heap.

Jesus told his seventy testifiers in Luke 10 to go out with nothing extra, nothing that they could hold over the people they were there to serve. Simplicity levels the playing field and teaches us to rely on the grace of God and the generosity of our unbelieving friends.

Think of it—a mission trip without credit cards, matching T-shirts, and a suitcase full of clothes and hygiene products! It was like Jesus was asking them to take a temporary vow of poverty as they went out to share his gospel. This was "the best way Jesus knew to move his followers into the arms of God," says Scott Bessenecker, "and bind them to the needy people who would welcome them."[116]

I'm not saying that destitution is a prerequisite for all good witnesses in every circumstance. But can you see that by making them leave everything behind Jesus highlighted their identification with the people he sent them to reach? He commissioned them as *incarnational* evangelists.

So, how does that affect our testimony? Total spiritual victory, complete physical health, an all-star family, and a respectable middle-class (or above) lifestyle is the image we prefer to project. Yet I propose that sometimes, the best witnesses are the neediest ones. Sometimes we have to be poor enough to reach other poor folks, where our loss is their gain.

The song we evangelizers like to sing goes something like this:

I have something that you don't…
I'm saved and you're lost…

> *All my needs and wants are met by God…*
> *Don't you wish you could be like me!*

I recommend some lyrics that sound more like:

> *I know what you're going through…*
> *Yeah, I'm hurting and confused too…*
> *I thought my life was totally over, but Jesus stays near…*
> *He loves me in spite of me…*
> *And I'm sure he loves you that way too!*

Our common life-wounds tend to bridge the gap between us. When we can identify with others' pain, they're more apt to take notice when we invite them into the Creator's circle of friends.

Furthermore he told them, *"Go! I am sending you out like lambs among wolves…"*[117] What kind of shepherd sends his sheep to be among wolves? Is it because we're "sheep with superpowers?" asks Neil Cole. "The difference is not in the sheep as much as in the Shepherd… We are no different from the lost sheep except that now we have a Shepherd—and what a difference he makes!"[118]

Jesus sent them out *vulnerable* as well as needy, which is how I imagine the scouts felt in Jericho. It sounds like a cockeyed approach for any enterprise, spiritual or otherwise. Most people don't like being needy or vulnerable, let alone do it on purpose and project it to their customers. Shouldn't we be the ones with all the answers and no questions? Self-assurance and strength is simple Marketing 101. Shocking as it is, the paternalistic approach hasn't endeared us to a needy world or won many converts!

Note this piece of Paul's newsletter from his first missions trip: *"As you know, it was because of an illness that I first preached the gospel to you, and even though my illness was a trial to you, you did not treat me with contempt or scorn. Instead, you welcomed me as if I were an angel of God, as if I were Christ Jesus himself. Where, then, is your blessing of me now? I can testify that, if you could have done so, you would have torn out your eyes and given them to me."*[119]

How's that for an account of the great Apostle's initial evangelistic tour? He got so sick that the people he was serving had to serve him! And yet he deemed his infirmity as an opportunity for his ministry. What we might regard a disadvantage became an advantage to his attempts at influencing people toward Christ in Galatia. Whatever medical condition he suffered from, instead of hindering the progress of his mission, it actually pushed it forward. His illness opened doors for him. As counterintuitive as it is, God often finesses our vulnerabilities into his strategy to use us in the greatest way possible.

Paul's second missions trip didn't go much differently when he arrived in Corinth shaking in his sandals. In his newsletter account of that trip, he writes: *"I came to you in weakness with great fear and trembling."*[120] Not your typical newsletter headline! But who wouldn't shudder at the thought of ministering in Corinth—a town not exactly known for its receptivity to the gospel? In fact, at one point, Paul even thought about tapping out when the Spirit came in to buoy his confidence.[121]

Joshua's two scouts, Jesus' seventy-member advance team, and the Apostle Paul all went out feebly. They shared their friendship with God with others, not so much in spite of their weakness, but through it. Rather than reducing its power, their frailty boosted the power of their testimony—and ours.

Approaching people as ferocious wolves rather than as vulnerable lambs may boost our ego, but it won't win many to the One who is "gentle and humble in heart."[122]

God chooses foolish things to shame the wise and weak things to shame the strong.[123] Rather than approaching people from the vantage point of proficiency, we're more apt to win them over as *one frail soul to another.*

A lot of Christians won't share their faith with people unless they have all their own personal problems solved and are armed to the teeth with answers to every question about God. They figure if they go out needy, no one will give them the time of day. They assume that if the *witness-ees* are better off than the *witnesses* (physically, emotionally, financially), they'll never be able to convince them to accept their invitation to follow Jesus. But nothing could be further from the truth.

It's not the person with the best life that necessarily has the best testimony. In fact, often it's the incurably cheerful Christian that is off-putting and comes across as disingenuous and condescending. While I admire the Super Bowl MVP when he gives praise to God on national TV for his athletic ability, I suspect that it's the faithful Jesus-following janitor who barely survives between paychecks that has the most impact on the people he meets.

People drawn only to MVP testimonies tend to come to Jesus for self-absorbed reasons, in hopes that he will make them successful too. If all they ever hear are anecdotes of triumph (whether accurately portrayed or hyperbolized), they will only seek him for what he can do to make them prosperous.

In addition to the stories of miraculous interventions, our testimony should include the times he didn't intervene in any observable way, but when he gently wept with us and gave us peace and helped us endure.

If we present God as the Great Fixer of problems, our "converts" might not ever fall in love with him, but only hang around faith just so they can use him. That sort of "MVP-Maker" testimony is a potential recipe for weak and mercenary "converts," ones prone to wander.

Maybe we should rethink our testimonies.

CONCLUSION

One Thing Leads To Another

> *"The life I touch for good or ill will touch another life, and that in turn another, until who knows where the trembling stops or in what far place my touch will be felt?"*
> — **Frederick Buechner**

Before "evangelism" was even a thing, before the people of God even thought of themselves as *friendship makers,* this story stealthily coaxes us toward complicity with God in his quest for friends. Even after reading this you still might not select Rahab's story as your first choice to inspire sharing Jesus with people. But hopefully, by looking beneath the surface of the narrative, you now have a template of how you might conduct yourself on our quest. God's passionate pursuit of such an unlikely candidate for conversion might well indicate a pattern, his modus operandi of reaching some of the least, last, and lost of his beloved lambs.

We're like scouts, sent by our "Joshua" to look for *Rahabs.* They might appear at first glance to be improbable *potential* followers of Jesus, let alone *influential* disciple-producing followers. But this story urges us to look past their off-putting exterior and lifestyle. It prompts us to listen for the song of the Spirit already resonating in their spirit, however faint it may be. By developing a sincere and reciprocal relationship with them and creatively communicating Jesus' love and sacrifice, we join in harmony with his song.

We promise her that if she will drape the redemptive red rope from her window, she will be rescued from destruction and welcomed into our community of faith with open arms. Then her influence will increase and generations to follow will be impacted to the glory of God!

The impact of reaching one who reaches another is viral. *"Teach these truths to other trustworthy people,"* says a famous mentor to his mentee, *"who will be able to pass them on to others."*[124]

Rahab isn't the only one saved in the story. She cuts a deal with Joshua's scouts to include her parents, siblings, and their families. It occurs to me that if all she cared about was her own salvation she would've simply gone back with the scouts when she first encountered them and left her family to die in the attack. It doesn't sound like it even entered her mind to leave her loved ones behind. Her first reflex is to bring them with her.

Think about it. The proverbial "black sheep"—the town prostitute—is the chief "witness" to her family! Even more unexpected, they promise that if they stay in her house of ill-repute, they will be saved from the impending disaster. That's another first. *You'll be saved if you're in a brothel when judgment comes!*

Rahab believes the scouts, and her family believes her. Yes, God does work in mysterious ways. *"Isn't it obvious,"* says Paul, *"that God deliberately chose men and women that the culture overlooks and exploits and abuses, chose these 'nobodies' to expose the hollow pretensions of the 'somebodies'?"*[125]

Rahab shows us how *not to* hoard our salvation. She instinctually shares it with those closest to her. The evangelized becomes the evangelizer. Jesus said that his followers intuitively fish for other followers.[126] The scouts "catch" Rahab, and she catches her family.

Pretty much all of Jesus' commands could be boiled down to three: *Love God, love people, and make disciples.* The first one is the "greatest," the second follows close behind,[127] and the third is what we've been talking about throughout this book.[128]

Lovers of God love people toward becoming God lovers themselves—"disciples."

He instructs us to "make disciples" not just *decisions.* This is the term many churches use when counting the number of people who respond to an evangelistic invitation. They say, *"There were a hundred decisions for Christ in the service last Sunday!"* It's not a term entirely without merit since saving faith does entail a decision, but the decision is only the beginning of the journey, not even close to the end.

Jesus goes on to say that we make disciples by *baptizing* those who have made a decision to follow Jesus and by *teaching* them to do everything he commanded, i.e. love God, love people, and make disciples. Hence, the disciples we make are to be the kind of disciples that make other disciples—*"disciple-making disciples."*

Don't get me wrong; helping someone come to Jesus, then another, and another is great. But it's even greater when we bring someone to him who then turns around and brings others to him.

New disciples are almost always the most effective in bringing their own loved ones into the divine friendship. A common mistake churches make is to extract and isolate new believers from their culture and indoctrinate them into our Christian subculture. By the time they get through with them, they might know the definitions of all the major themes of the Bible, but they're too detached from their world that they no longer have any influence there. Rahab, on the other hand, wins her own family in her own home.

Like ripples in a pond, the sphere of Christ's saving influence expands outward— from the scouts to Rahab and then to her immediate family members. But wait, there's more, much more. As previously noted, Rahab went on to marry into the Jewish tribe of Judah, and then four generations later, her great-great-grandson, David, was born. That's what I call ripples of influence rolling outward! Perhaps David grew up hearing stories of his relative, the pagan prostitute, and how she came to believe in Yahweh.

And, even more scandalous, this puts Rahab in the lineage of King Jesus—"a woman of the night," grafted into the family tree of the Son of God. The scouts reached her, she reached her family, she married a godly man, and the rest, as they say, is history. One thing really does lead to another!

When we help someone find Jesus, we never know how far those ripples will travel beyond our own place and time. Reach a *Rahab* and we have no idea what sort of kingdom chain of events our efforts may instigate.

Rahab lives and works and plays somewhere in your sphere of influence. She may not look to you like the "sort" of person likely to become a follower of Jesus, but that's the magnificence of

God's quest for friends. How would we ever experience that magnificence if we aren't willing to look past her exterior and delve into what's beneath?

If an old tarnished, limping lover of God like me can be a friend of God, let alone one who makes friends along with God, so can you.

Recommended Reading

Evangelism

- Everts, Don and Schaupp, Doug. *I Once Was Lost: What Postmodern Skeptics Taught Us About Their Path to Jesus* (InterVarsity Press, 2008)
- Kimball, Dan. *They Like Jesus But Not The Church: Insights from Emerging Generations* (Zondervan, 2007)
- Hunter, George G. *The Celtic Way of Evangelism: How Christianity Can Reach the West,* (Abingdon Press, 2000)
- Henderson, Jim. *Evangelism Without Additives (Waterbrook Press, 2007)*
- Medearis, Carl. *Speaking of Jesus, The Art of Not-Evangelism* (David C. Cook, 2011)

Prevenient Grace

- Richardson, Don. *Eternity in Their Hearts* (Regal Books, 1984)
- Sanders, John. *No Other Name: An Investigation Into the Destiny of the Unevangelized,* (Eerdmans Publishing, 1992)

- Pinnock, Clark. *A Wideness in God's Mercy: The Finality Of Jesus Christ In A World Of Religions* (Zondervan, 1992)
- Jones, E. Stanley. *The Christ Of The Mount: A Working Philosophy Of Life* (Andesite Press, 2017)

Apologetics

- Strobel, Lee. *The Case for Christ* (Zondervan, 1998)
- Strobel, Lee. *The Case for Faith* (Zondervan, 2009)
- Keller, Tim. *The Reason for God* (Penguin Books, 2009)
- Lewis, C.S. *Mere Christianity* (Harper Collins, 1943)
- McDowell, Sean. *Apologetics For A New Generation* (Harvest House Publishers, 2009)
- Boyd, Gregory. *Is God To Blame?* (InterVarsity Press, 2003)
- Zacharias, Ravi. *The End of Reason: A Response to the New Atheists* (Zondervan, 2008)

The Gospel to the Poor

- Stearns, Richard. *The Hole in Our Gospel* (Thomas Nelson, 2009)
- Martin, Jim. *The Just Church: Becoming a Risk-Taking, Justice-Seeking, Disciple-Making Congregation* (Tyndale, 2012)
- Keller, Tim. *Generous Justice: How God's Grace Makes Us Just* (Penguin Books, 2010)
- Heuertz, Christopher. *Friendship at the Margins: Discovering Mutuality in Service and Mission* (Intervarsity Press, 2010)
- Borthwick, Paul. *Great Commission, Great Compassion* (InterVarsity Press, 2015)

- Corbett, Steve; Fikkert, Brian. *When Helping Hurts: How to Alleviate Poverty Without Hurting the Poor . . . and Yourself* (Moody Publishers, 2012)
- Bessenecker, Scott. *The New Friars: The Emerging Movement Serving the World's Poor* (InterVarsity Press, 2006)

For Personal Reflection, Group Discussion, and Taking Action

I trust that you have a friend or a small group that you meet with for spiritual support and accountability. If not, you should get one. You might like to work through this book together, discuss its contents, pray with each other for people *(Rahabs)* you're trying to reach, and hold each other accountable. As with pretty much any aspect of our life in Jesus, we're more likely to actually move on what we believe if we have someone else to "spur us on to love and good deeds." (Hebrews 10:24)

That said, one weakness with meeting and discussing spiritual truth—and even praying about it—is our tendency to feel as though by doing so we've acted on it. Talking and praying about doing something is not the same as doing it. Bible studies and prayer groups *without works are dead*—or something like that! I hope this book will get you talking and praying with people about talking to people about Jesus, and then actually talking to people who need Jesus.

Introduction

Don't Fight the Force

- On the spectrum of *adventure* versus *personal security* what are you looking for in your relationship with God? Be honest now!

    (Security) 1 – 2 – 3 – 4 – 5 – 6 – 7 – 8 – 9 – 10 (Adventure)

- How does your perspective on sharing Jesus with people factor into this?

- Does the thought of sharing Jesus bring up guilty feelings in you? Short of just giving up, what can you do to allay those feelings?

The Friendship Quest

- Are you naturally "bold" in your interaction with others about Jesus? How much do you think it matters?

- What do you think about the proposal that "witnesses are *what we are*, not simply something *we do*"? And how does this impact the way you might approach "witnessing"?

- Enter the name of someone in your phone or journal that you would like to coax closer to Jesus. Share this with a friend to join you in prayer.

Expertise Not Required

- In what period of your life since meeting Jesus have you had the most passion and effectiveness in "good newsing" your friends and family? How can you retain or recover that passion?

- If "gospeling" doesn't belong exclusively to the professionals (evangelists and all manner of preacher types), what do you have to offer that maybe they do not?

- What is the essence of "the gospel of Jesus"? How can you share at least one piece of it this week with someone? [Don't forget the person from the previous chapter that you put in your phone or journal.]

Reaching Rahab

- Okay, I admit that the Rahab story is a pretty random one on which to base a discussion on evangelism, but give it time. I think the rationale for it will gradually unfold. It would help if you took the time to read Joshua 2 and 6, if not the entire first six chapters.

- If Rahab represents marginalized or otherwise disregarded folks in our lives, write the names of three people in your circle of influence who fit that description.

- Which one of those three will you make some effort to further your friendship with this week? How will you do it?

PART ONE – A Supernaturally Installed Wonder

- Recall a Rea Sea crossing story of your own. Pray now for at least one divine appointment with a not-yet-Christian person this week and tell it.

- Cite a friend of yours that already has "a pretty good idea of who God is" even without any Christian influence in their life. If not from Sunday School, the Bible, or a Christian, where did they got that idea?

- If there is a spark of spiritual revelation in that person, ask God to open a door for you to "speak to the spark" this week.

God's Passionate Pursuit of People

- What "cameo appearances" did God make in your story before you came to Jesus? What are some typical ones you've heard from other unbelievers?

- Think about and/or discuss the statement: "… in some cases what we call 'evangelism' is little more than a simple confirmation of what God has already put in their heart, whether they know it or not."

- How is the "Great Commission" *great?* And how is it a *"co-mission"*?

She Sees God in Creation

- Read Psalm 19:1-6 and Romans 1:19-20 and identify at least five aspects of creation that make atheism a pretty hard sell.

- Which aspects of God's creation are most likely to speak to your not-yet-Christian friends? Ask the Spirit to turn up the volume of his communication to them today.

- How can you help someone draw a causal line from creation to the Creator? Pray for wisdom and the opportunity to do it this week.

She Sees God in Her Conscience

- Read Romans 2:14-16. What does this mean about your friends who have had no religious background or exposure to the teachings of the Bible?

- What does this mean about someone's claim that there are no moral absolutes and that everything is "relative"?

- How can you take advantage of the reality of this "inside information about God" in your "good newsing" of your friends? Be on the alert for opportunities this week.

She Sees God in Her Culture

- Think of a friend that you hope to point toward Jesus. What aspects of their culture most directly reveal God to them?

- What does the "relational code" installed in our DNA do to attract people to God?

- What toxic aspects of our dysfunctional culture might you cite in conversations with people in order to point them toward "the better society" (the kingdom of God)?

She Sees God in Her Crises

- Give an example of someone you know who came to Jesus as a direct result of a crisis in their life.

- No doubt you know someone in your sphere of influence that is going through a crisis right now. How can you serve them in the name of Jesus? Unless checked by the Spirit, what are you waiting for? Go ahead and do it.

- I proposed that warning them about hell (the "ultimate crisis") is not usually the most effective approach to entice people to Christ these days. In what circumstances have you found it unavoidable to bring judgment into the conversation?

She Sees God in Her Creed

- Review John 14:6; Acts 4:12; and 1 Timothy 2:5. How is Jesus unique among all the other prophets and founders of religions?

- What common ground have you encountered in conversations with people from other religions (i.e., moral values, forgiveness, peace…)?

- Do you have a friend who is a devotee of another spiritual tradition? (If not, it's possible you don't get out enough and talk to people unlike yourself. Just sayin'.) If you do have such a friend, how can you engage in redemptive conversations with him/her by building on things you agree upon?

Enter – A Pair of "Witnesses"

- If people are being "pre-evangelized" by creation, conscience, culture, etc.; what do we have to offer that they don't? In other words, what can you do to show and share God that the galaxy cannot?

- Read 1 Peter 3:15. Describe the "hope" you possess since coming to Christ. How can you share it with not-yet-Jesus-lovers?

- Name one friend that has "pockets full of God invitations" but either doesn't *recognize them* or doesn't *understand them?* What can you do to identify and clarify them? Ask the Father for a divine appointment so you can practice this week.

We'll Take That "To Go"

- If there is such a thing as a *"Supernaturally Installed Wonder,"* how does it allay our *rush* to push people to conversion?

- If you believe the Spirit has gone out in front of us to befriend people, how does it help you to be *"less scripted in your efforts and a little more agile in your interactions"*?

- *"God loves people way too much to hinge their eternal destiny on the quality of your performance."* Does that help you be more *yourself* when you share Jesus with people? How?

- Before moving on to Part Two, make a list of at least three people you want to nudge toward Jesus. Pray for them daily and ask a Christian friend to pray with you. Ask them also to follow up with you as time progresses.

PART TWO – Accidental Evangelism

- Cite a recent *"Eternally Ordained Opportunity"* of yours where God put someone in your path for you to share his good news.

- What unbelieving person is in your circle of influence right now whose *hidden eternal treasure* (Proverbs 20:5) is obvious to you but not yet to him or her? Ask the Lord for wisdom about how to share with them.

- While you might be more geared to hear the Spirit's love song to *you,* ask him to help you hear the song he's singing to your pre-christian friends.

The Wordless Witness

- How does improving your listening to what others have to say increase your chances of saying what they need to hear?

- Unpack Henderson's quote: *"We should preach as though we're serving and serve as though we're preaching."*

- *"Whether or not they realize it, everyone has an internal need to belong."* Who do you know that has an obvious need to "belong"? What can/will you do to include them in your life and community?

The Disarming Power of Reluctant Humility

- Read 1 Peter 3:15 again and hone in on "gentleness and respect." How are these essential to effective "good newsing"?

- Ask the Spirit to root out pride and paternalism in your heart and replace them with humility and a spirit of servanthood.

- Describe an incident where the person you were sharing Jesus with was more full of his/her spirits than you were of the Holy Spirit. What can/will you do to fix that next time?

Sometimes Less is More

- Is it true that being silver-tongued and skillful can at times actually *"inhibit the Spirit's efforts to find his way into a person's consciousness"*? Why or why not?

- Do you agree that an *"information-heavy"* approach is not always the best way to witness? Why or why not?

- When is "apologetics" a good approach to take? In order to be a more effective witness what issues would you like to be more conversant in? How will you get that knowledge? (See the "Apologetics" section in Recommended Reading for starters.)

PART THREE – It Takes a Savior To Save

- Read Mark 4: 26-29 again. Pay attention to these phrases: "*whether he sleeps or gets up, the seed sprouts and grows, though he does not know how... All by itself the soil produces grain...*" How do they apply to our seed planting efforts?

- Read Romans 1:16-17 and meditate on or discuss with a friend the following: "*... we should give the gospel itself and our personal story a little more credit, and the Spirit's serenade a little more opportunity to find its way into their consciousness.*"

- Do you agree that God wants everyone to be saved and that salvation is a supernatural act and that prayer is one of our most powerful tools to unleash the supernatural? If so, commit to pray for at least one pre-saved friend for at least the next week to come to Jesus.

Savior Sellers?

- "Tour Guides... Matchmakers... Show & Tell..." Choose one of these metaphors about sharing the life of Jesus with people and elaborate on it.

- Which one is the most vivid to you of how we should witness and why? Do you have a different metaphor in mind?

- Imagine yourself as a tour guide, matchmaker, or kid doing show & tell with a particular unbelieving person in your sphere of influence and pray for an opportunity to do what you imagine this week.

Winning, Not Wounding

- *"Sometimes we Christians forget who the enemy is and we attack the hostages rather than the hostage takers."* Agree or disagree? Give examples.

- *"Compassionate service wields a power to affect people in ways that argumentative tactics never can."* Share an example of how true this is and find a way this week to show compassionate service to someone in need.

- After blowing it the first time, Peter got a second chance with Malchus (through his nephew). Is there someone you'd like another chance at showing and sharing Jesus to? Ask the Spirit for help to do it better next time.

Sometimes Do and Sometimes Don't

- Why would it be helpful to acknowledge that there's more than one brand of "lostness"?

- If Jesus' approach to telling the good news suited the circumstance and the person, how much more should you and

I be flexible in our presentation of him? Recount an instance when you shared the good news in an unconventional way.

- Unpack this statement: *"Being the one Christian they've ever talked with that didn't go into a fevered sales pitch might just be the best thing we can do for this particular God-loved soul at the time."*

The "Jesus Bus"

- Unpack the idea that there are "buses" (religions) that travel in the general direction of God. They won't take people *all the way* there, but they might deposit them closer to him than when they began their trip. Do you know someone for whom this was true?

- What benefit is there in identifying common ground with people of other faiths? Is it helpful to locate "traces of truth" in their religious systems rather than expending all our energy tearing down the fallacies of their beliefs?

- Instead of debating with people about comparative religion, tell them what you know to be true about him and why you love him so much. Pray with a friend about doing just that this week.

Rahab's Redemptive Red Rope

- Ask the Lord to help you notice the creative means (i.e., a red rope) he places in front of you to share the salvation story.

- *"What can wash away my sin? Nothing but the blood of Jesus."* The cross is the crux of the gospel. How do you typically share the message of the cross with pre-christians?

- *"It's the rope that saves, not how well we comprehend it."* That goes for both evangelizers and the evangelized? How encouraging is this and why?

PART FOUR – Befriending the Prostituted

- Jesus: Scandalously loving and violator of social taboos. True or False? Examples?

- Consider John Burke's *mud-covered Rembrandt* metaphor. *"Do you see the mud or the masterpiece?"* What is your honest answer?

- Are you currently befriending a person that, if you brought them to your church, would stand out like a sore thumb and might be stared at or otherwise made to feel less than entirely welcome? Give it a shot and see what happens.

Humanizing the Dehumanized

- How familiar are you with human trafficking and what it does to the humans God loves? Check out one or more of these sources of information on abolitionism for victims and aftercare of survivors: *Not For Sale* by David Batstone, *FreedomHouseSF.org*, *The Slave Next Door* by Kevin Bales. Ask God how he wants you to invest yourself in solutions.

- "People dehumanize one another in ways other than sexual exploitation—child and spousal abuse, racism, classism, and gender bias to name a few." Who do you know in one or more of those categories of objectification or oppression and how can you share some hope with them?

- Everyone needs human warmth, especially those damaged by abuse or marginalization. What can you do to be a person safe enough for them to give human connection a try?

Re-earning Trust

- A lot of people think Christians are *"angry, judgmental, right-wing finger-pointers with political agendas..."* Is this true? Before answering too quickly, ask a pre-christian what they think of us?

- We've got lots of work to do to re-earn people's trust in Christ followers. Though you can't singlehandedly transform our reputation in the world, what good works can/will you do to chip away at their negative perception?

- Unpack the statement: *"Good witnesses are safe people with a dangerous message."* As a witness, how can you personally be "safe" and "dangerous" at the same time?

Mutualizing the Marginalized

- What do you think of Christopher Heuertz' following statement? *"A focus on friendship [with the poor] rearranges our assumptions. What if the resources they have also meet our needs? What if Jesus is already present in ways that will minister to us? What if in sharing life together as friends we all move closer to Jesus' heart?"*

- Name a person outside your *"comfort zone of commonality"*—someone unlike you socio-economically, ethnically, or culturally—that you want to befriend. If no such person comes to mind, be in the hunt for one.

- As a *"friend of sinners,"* Jesus enjoyed their friendship maybe as much as they did his. It's apparent that they brought something of value to the relationship. What do Rahab-like people contribute to your two-way street relationship with them?

Outer Circle Christians

- Though God doesn't specifically assign everyone to focus on the disadvantaged, there are some good reasons to include people outside our own socioeconomic demographic in our friendship making. What are those reasons?

- Jesus wants our perimeter to be "porous and penetrable in order to include castoffs." On a scale of 1 to 10 how "porous" is your perimeter? How about your church's perimeter? What can/will you do about it?

- Read Luke 15:8-10. What trashed-yet-treasured person in your sphere of influence comes to mind and heart? Ask the Lord for an opportunity to reach out to them.

Squeezing Camels

- Obviously God doesn't love the poor and powerless more than the rich and powerful, so why does he seem to encourage us to give more attention to the former in our efforts to "gospel" them?

- Jesus indicates that some of the poor need a firmer nudge to come into the kingdom ("Make them come in."). Why is that, and what does that nudge look like?

- If you don't have immediate access to anyone with a less advantaged socioeconomic status than yours, get outside your neighborhood once in a while and make at least one friend. Know them by name, become familiar with what makes them unique among God's beloveds, share your story with them, and see what happens.

Rethinking Our Testimony

- What do you think of this statement: *"People drawn only to MVP testimonies tend to come to Jesus for self-absorbed reasons, in hopes that he will make them successful too. If all they ever hear are anecdotes of triumph (whether accurately portrayed or hyperbolized), they will only seek him for what he can do to make them prosperous."*

- I confessed that, *"one of the best things that ever happened to my testimony to needy people was to become needy myself."* Give an example from your own life how suffering helps you share the gospel with others. Why do you think that is?

- What will it take for you to be more *vulnerable* in your own testifying to God's grace? The next time you share Jesus with someone plan for it to look a little more like *"one frail soul to another."*

CONCLUSION – One Thing Leads To Another

- Read 2 Timothy 2:2 and identify the four consecutive spiritual generations Paul refers to. *Adding* a person to the kingdom is good; *multiplying* disciples is better. How does this affect your efforts in sharing the gospel with people?

- *"Reach a Rahab and we have no idea what sort of kingdom chain of events our efforts may instigate."* Those people with whom you are currently trying to introduce to Jesus have their own sphere of influence. Help them not only see their need to become a friend of God but to embrace the adventure of joining God's quest for more friends.

- *Rahab* does indeed live and work and play somewhere in your sphere of influence. I trust that you will find her, befriend her, offer Jesus to her, and let the Spirit do his thing. Welcome to the quest!

Acknowledgements

At the risk of sounding pretentious, I can't help but begin by acknowledging Jesus Christ. It stands to reason that I can't very well share the Savior without having a Savior to share! Plus, I like to believe that he's the One who, to at least some degree, forms my ideas about him and leads me in my attempts to share him with others. I owe everything—not just the contents of this book—to him.

My sincere thanks also to Karen and Dan for their longsuffering edits of my manuscript. If not for them, this would be a typo-filled, disjointed, and difficult read.

Thanks to my true evangelist friends, Edmond, Paul, Danny, Steve, and a number of others who inspire me in the friendship quest. Their relentless love for God and for people rouse the spirit inside me to be more like them.

Thanks to my street ministry partners who allow me to serve alongside them in the *Outer Circle* (Claire, John, Elizabeth, Matt, Brian, Hugh, and Megan) and in *Calvary Street Ministries* (Liz, Elijah, Matthew, Mark, Hugh, Rory, Matt, and Alison).

I thank also the multitude of unbelieving folks who have put up with my inadequate attempts to show and share Jesus with them. I thank them for listening in spite of my mistakes and for considering joining me in the adventure.

A final shout out to my precious children (Luke and Rebecca), their spouses (Tori and Casey), and my magnificent granddaughters (Aria and Esmé)!

About the Author

Barney Wiget started following Jesus in northern California during the Jesus Movement in the 1970s. He planted and pastored three churches on the California coast for over thirty years. He now lives in San Francisco as a self-proclaimed "vagabond preacher." In addition to making disciples and serving cultural castoffs he advocates for an aftercare home for human trafficking survivors called *Freedom House* (http://www.freedomhousesf.org/). He also writes for his blog, website and podcast.

Website and blog: barneywiget.com

Podcast: soundcloud.com/musingthemysteries

Memoir: *The Other End of the Dark: A Memoir About Divorce, Cancer, and Things God Does Anyway* available on Amazon.

Half of the profits from this book are donated to the San Francisco Youth With A Mission building fund (https://www.ywam-sanfrancisco.org/).

NOTES

Introduction
1. Carl Medearis, *Speaking of Jesus, The Art of Not-Evangelism* (David C. Cook, 2011)

2. Matthew 28:19-20

3. John 15:14

4. Richard J. Mouw. *Uncommon Decency: Christian Civility in an Uncivil World.* (InterVarsity Press, 2009)

5. Jim Henderson, *Evangelism Without Additives* (Waterbrook Press, 2007)

6. Ibid.

7. Matthew 1:5; Hebrews 11:31; James 2:25

PART ONE – A Supernaturally Installed Wonder
8. Clark Pinnock, *A Wideness in God's Mercy: The Finality Of Jesus Christ In A World Of Religions* (Zondervan, 1992)

9. Ecclesiastes 3:11

10. Joshua 2:11

11. 2 Peter 3:9

God's Passionate Pursuit of People

12. Psalm 19:4

13. 2 Corinthians 6:1

14. Matthew 11:29-30

15. Job 38:1

16. Numbers 2:9

17. Genesis 20:6

18. Matthew 2:1

19. Acts 10:2

20. Luke 15:4

21. John 1:9

22. John 5:17

23. John 12:32

24. John 16:8

25. Acts 14:17

26. Revelation 22:17

She Sees God in Creation
27. Romans 1:19

28. John 1:9

29. Romans 1:18

She Sees God in Her Conscience
30. C.S. Lewis, *Mere Christianity* (Harper Collins, 1943)

31. 2 Corinthians 13:1

32. Richard J. Mouw. *Uncommon Decency: Christian Civility in an Uncivil World.* (InterVarsity Press, 2009)

She Sees God in Her Crises
33. C.S. Lewis, *The Problem of Pain* (Harper Collins, 1940)

34. Joshua 6:23

She Sees God in Her Creed
35. C.S. Lewis, *Mere Christianity* (Harper Collins, 1943)

36. Don Richardson, *Eternity in Their Hearts* (Regal Books, 1984)

37. Mouw. *Uncommon Decency*

38. John 14:6; Acts 4:12; 1 Timothy 2:5

"I am the way and the truth and the life. No one comes to the Father except through me."

"Salvation is found in no one else, for there is no other name under heaven given to mankind by which we must be saved."

"For there is one God and one mediator between God and mankind, the man Christ Jesus."

39. Hebrews 1:1-4

40. E. Stanley Jones, *The Christ Of The Mount: A Working Philosophy Of Life* (Andesite Press, 2017)

41. 1 Corinthians 9:21-23 (The Message)

Enter – A Pair of "Witnesses"

42. Revelation 22:17

43. To the pagans in Lystra, Paul said: *"[God] has not left himself without testimony."* And then he said what that testimony is comprised of: *"He has shown kindness by giving you rain from heaven and crops in their seasons; he provides you with plenty of food and fills your hearts with joy."* (Acts 14:17)

Rain, crops, food, and joyful hearts, they all "testify." (The term he used here is the same one Jesus used in the Great Commission, "…you shall be my *witnesses*.") So, God witnesses through his generous provision, and when we jump into the mix we're just adding our *witness* to his *witness!*

"How can they believe in the one of whom they have not heard?" Paul asked. *"And how can they hear without someone preaching to them?"* (Romans 10:14)

When Peter went to Cornelius' house, his hearers were so ready that they were receiving Jesus and being filled with the Holy Spirit before he could even finish his sermon (Acts 10).

Paul began his sermon in Athens by acknowledging what they already knew about God and built on that:

"I see that in every way you are very religious. For as I walked around and looked carefully at your objects of worship, I even found an altar with this inscription: TO AN UNKNOWN GOD. So you are ignorant of the very thing you worship— and this is what I am going to proclaim to you." (Acts 17:23) He affirms that they are seeking after God and honors them for wanting to worship something.

44. 1 Peter 3:15

We'll Take That "To Go"
45. Romans 1:16

46. Romans 1:14

PART TWO – Accidental Evangelism
47. Ephesians 2:10

48. Proverbs 20:5

The Wordless Witness
49. Jude 22

50. Luke 8:18

51. Romans 6:13

52. Matthew 5:16

53. 1 Peter 2:12

54. Matthew 5:9

55. Matthew 1:5

56. John 3:8

57. Matthew 1:5

58. John 13:35

The Disarming Power of Reluctant Humility
59. You can find my book, *The Other End of the Dark* on Amazon. The proceeds go to a safe house for trafficking survivors called Freedom House.

60. 1 Peter 3:15

Sometimes Less is More

61. Joshua 6:10

62. Don Everts and Doug Schaupp, *I Once Was Lost (Downers Grove, IL InterVarsity Press, 2008)*

63. 1 Peter 3:15

64. Sean McDowell, *Apologetics for a New Generation* (Harvest House Publishers, 2009)

65. Everts and Schaupp, *I Once Was Lost*

PART THREE – It Takes a Savior To Save

66. John 1:41-42

67. Henderson, *Evangelism Without Additives*

68. 1 John 1:2-3

69. 2 Corinthians 5:20

70. John 4:29

71. John 10:9

72. Joshua 2:15

73. Romans 1:16-17

Savior Sellers?
74. Dan Kimball, *They Like Jesus but Not the Church: Insights from Emerging Generations* (Zondervan, 2007)

75. Medearis, *Speaking of Jesus*

Winning, Not Wounding
76. Everts and Schaupp, *I Once Was Lost*

77. Gregory A. Boyd, *Benefit of the Doubt: Breaking the Idol of Certainty* (Baker Publishing Group, 2013)

78. Medearis, *Speaking of Jesus*

79. Henderson, *Evangelism Without Additives*

80. McDowell, *Apologetics for a New Generation*

81. Matthew 5:44

82. Matthew 26:41

83. John 18:26

84. John 21:15-17

85. 1 Peter 3:15 (The Message)

Sometimes Do and Sometimes Don't
86. Proverbs 11:30

87. Luke 19:10

88. Henderson, *Evangelism Without Additives*

The "Jesus Bus"
89. E. Stanley Jones, *The Christ Of The Mount*

90. Mark 12:34

Rahab's Redemptive Red Rope
91. Job 9:33 (ESV)

92. 1 Timothy 2:5

93. 1 John 2:2

94. Isaiah 55:9

95. Genesis 38:27-30

PART FOUR – Befriending the Prostituted
96. 2 Samuel 12:24

97. Ronald J. Sider, *Just Generosity: A New Vision for Overcoming Poverty in America* (Baker Books, 1999, 2007)

Humanizing the Dehumanized

98. Christopher Heuertz, *Friendship at the Margins: Discovering Mutuality in Service and Mission* (Intervarsity Press, 2010)

99. John 4:1ff

100. John 4:41

101. Revelation 18:13

102. Traffickers and all manner of abusers throw vulnerable human beings into a sewage filled river for their own financial benefit. Abolitionism consists of prevention, intervention, and aftercare. God places some people upstream to keep others from being abused to begin with, some midstream to pull them out, and some downstream to give them CPR and wash them clean. Problem is, even when they get away from the smell, it remains in their smeller.

    Can you imagine what PTSD plagues the mind of the survivor of such trauma—the shame, fear, distrust, self-loathing, the anxiety? Frankly, I hope you can't. The kind of damage done to the human psyches of trafficked humans from relentless and long-term abuse only God can sort out. But he uses people to help people.

    There are a number of ministries that, by compassionate aftercare, "humanize the dehumanized" for victims of human trafficking. I work with one such Christ-centered home survivors called Freedom House located in the San Francisco Bay Area. I commend them to you for prayers, volunteer opportunities, and donations.

Re-earning Trust
103. Kimball, *They Like Jesus but Not the Church*

104. Everts and Schaupp, *I Once Was Lost*

105. Kimball, *They Like Jesus but Not the Church*

106. I'm indebted to Dan Kimball's thoughts and diagrams on this idea: Kimball, *They Like Jesus but Not the Church*

Mutualizing the Marginalized
107. Matthew 11:19

108. John 4:7

109. Heuertz, *Friendship at the Margins*

110. Ibid.

111. Richard Stearns, *The Hole in Our Gospel* (Thomas Nelson, 2009)

112. Luke 15:8-10

Outer Circle Christians
113. Romans 1:14

Squeezing Camels
114. Acts 1:8

115. Luke 14:16-24

116. Scott Bessenecker, *The New Friars: The Emerging Movement Serving the World's Poor* (InterVarsity Press, 2006)

Rethinking Our Testimony
117. Luke 10:3

118. Neil Cole, *Organic Church* (Jossey-Bass, 2009)

119. Galatians 4:13-15

120. 1 Corinthians 2:3

121. Acts 18:9-10

122. Matthew 11:29

123. 1 Corinthians 1:27

CONCLUSION – One Thing Leads To Another
124. 2 Timothy 2:2 (NLT)

125. 1 Corinthians 1:28 (The Message)

126. Matthew 4:19

127. Matthew 22:37-39

128. Matthew 28:19-20

BARNEY WIGET

… REACHING RAHAB

REACHING RAHAB

Made in the USA
Lexington, KY
11 May 2019